MATTHEW HALL

I0145816

Dark Psychology

Your Great Manual To Learn All The Dark Techniques Of Dark Psychology And Manipulation And Understand Mind Control, Hypnosis And NLP

Copyright © 2020 Matthew Hall

Table of Content

Introduction

I t is the study of the human condition because it involves people's psychological nature; that is, they prey on other people with criminal activities and criminal motives. Illegal reasons and unlawful purposes lack instinct and social science theories. All human beings may harm other humans and creatures. Although many people have suppressed or sublimated this trend, some have acted on these impulses. Dark psychology attempts to understand the thoughts, feelings, perceptions, and subjective processing systems that lead to predatory behavior contrary to the contemporary understanding of human behavior. Dark psychology assumes that crime, deviance, and abuse are purposeful and have rational, goal-oriented motivation 99.99% of the time. It is the remaining 0.01% of the dark psychology part of Adler's theory and teleology. Dark psychology assumes an area in the human mind that enables some people to perform cruel behavior without a purpose. In this theory, it is called a dark singularity.

Dark psychology believes that all humanity's malicious intentions towards others vary from minimal ambiguous and short thoughts to purely psychotic deviant behavior, without any rationality of cohesion. That is called a dark continuum. Dark psychology calls it the confounding factor. The mitigating factor is the promoter and attractant close to the mysterious singularity. The heinous behavior of people falls on the dark continuum. A brief introduction to these concepts is as follows. Dark psychology is a concept that the author has struggled with for fifteen years. It was only recently that he finally conceptualized the human condition, philosophy, and psychology definition. Dark psychology covers all the people who connect us to the dark side. All cultures, all faiths, and all humanity suffer from this well-known cancer. From the moment we are born to our death, there is a latent side within us, which some people call evil. In contrast, others define it as crime, immorality, and pathology.

Dark Psychology introduces a third philosophical construction, arguing that these behaviors are different from religious teachings and contemporary social science theories. Dark psychology believes that some people will act the same, not for power, money, gender, retribution, or any other known purpose. They commit these terrible acts without aim. Simply put, their use does not justify their methods. Some people assault and hurt others because of this. There is this potential in all of us. The area the author explores may be to harm others for no reason, no explanation, or purposelessness. Dark psychology believes that this dark potential is very complicated and even confusing to define. Dark psychology assumes that we all have the potential for predator behavior and that this potential can enter our thoughts, feelings, and perceptions. As you will read through this manual, we all have this potential, but only a few of us will make a difference. All of us once had the thought and feeling of acting cruelly. All of us have thought about hurting others seriously and without mercy.

You are honest with yourself. You have to agree with the thoughts and feelings you once thought about committing heinous behavior. Given this fact, we consider ourselves to be a kind species. We want to believe that these thoughts and feelings do not exist. Unfortunately, we all have these ideas, and fortunately, no action has taken against them. Dark psychology constitutes that some people have the same thoughts, feelings, and opinions but act deliberately or impulsively. The apparent difference is that they operate independently, while others only have brief thoughts and feelings about it. "Dark Psychology" believes that this

6

predator style is purposeful and has a specific rational, goal-oriented motivation. Religion, philosophy, psychology, and other dogmas have made convincing attempts to define dark psychology. Most human behaviors related to evil practices are indeed purposeful and goal-oriented. Still, dark psychology believes that persistent behavior and goal-oriented motives seem to be blurred in a particular field.

From thought to pure psychosis, dark psychology has suffered continuous damage without any apparent rationality or purpose. This continuum, the dark continuum, helps conceptualize the philosophy of dark psychology. Dark psychology addresses human psychology or the general human condition that allows or might even promote predatory behavior. In many cases, this behavioral tendency's specific characteristics lack the rational motivation of universality and predictability. Dark psychology believes that this general human condition is different or an extension of evolution. Let's look at some basic principles of development. First of all, consider that we have evolved from other animals. At present, we are a model of all animal life. Our frontal lobe makes us apex creatures. Now let us suppose that being advanced creatures does not entirely separate us from animals' instincts and predatory nature.

Chapter 1. What Is Dark Psychology?

T he idea of psychology is to help people by helping them understand themselves. Dark psychology is about using the mental weaknesses that people have to get people to do what you want them to do. I know it sounds cringe worth to many people, but this is not nearly as bad as you think it is. The fact is that everywhere around, the tools of dark psychology are chipping away at your mind. Facebook ran a test on its users by curating their content and measuring their mood. They wanted to see how showing people more negative content would affect their news by showing them more positive content. Magazines and advertisements like to play on your need to keep up with the Joneses or not lose something. In doing so, you are drawn into whatever they are selling. The news feeds a looping heap of controlled opinions to try and make you agree with the viewpoint you already share. The world is full of psychology being used darkly, and most of the time, you are on the receiving end of it rather than getting the benefit of it.

That is about to change. Dark Psychology is about recognizing the compulsions, needs, and desires that we all have, which can be used to get what we want.

What Do We Mean by That?

Whether it is a fear of loss, a desire to keep up with the Joneses, or a need to feel wanted or feel right, these things guide our decisions and impulses, whether we like them or not.

Alternatively, whether we want them to or not, people act against their interests every day simply because they are in an emotional state that guides your actions. When someone finds out these emotional triggers, it is a matter of time before they can start to guide your actions, control your behavior, and even manipulate you.

There can be nothing worse when people have figured out your emotional triggers and begin to play them. Whether it is a parent or a stranger, you can feel yourself often taking action and not even certain why you feel drawn to taking action just knowing that you have to, or want to, or that it is something that must be done. No, you cannot wait and Dark Psychology is the tool that sets this into action. It is the tool that shines a light on finding all these mental triggers in yourself and others.

It also recognizes that as amazing as our brains are, they take many shortcuts in the name of efficiency, which leaves them vulnerable to some of the simplest attacks. Ideally, our minds should not make us feel sad simply because we had a negative thought, and yet, this happens all the time. We're wandering around, having a good time, a good day. Someone says something or does something, maybe even inconsequential, and yet suddenly, our mood is shifted, and we have to fight to get back to balance. Our brains, however, are just working to be efficient; they are not working to be perfect. And when you understand that, you know that there is a huge opportunity to be had when dealing with people. More importantly, you understand that there are something's that you need to learn to safeguard yourself.

You have desires and wants, needs, and how far you are willing to go to have those things met. Do you know? What are your buying triggers? What are your emotional triggers? You have them, but are you completely aware of them. What makes you stressed, confused, angry, happy, and excited? All of these things are inside

9

your mind? They are inside everyone's mind. When you know how to access them, you will suddenly have greater freedom, happiness, excitement, and possibility in yourself and others. Because finally, you will be bringing your desires to life by getting others to see and want to help.

We are going to address manipulation—one of the keys to dark psychology. Manipulation is different from persuasion, influence, sales, and other such things. It is often about getting people to take action by playing on their weaknesses. We will talk about the ethics of manipulation, what you need to think about, and the "Right now" is essential to set the stage for what you can expect and learn the handful of psychological techniques and methods that will allow you to control people.

Dark Psychology is a tool, like a hammer. You can use it to build things or use it as a weapon to hurt people. We are making no moral judgments and go about using these skills. But the most important thing is for you to learn these techniques to make sure that you have a better understanding of yourself and what people are using against you.

The world can be a dangerous place knowing these techniques and understanding how people can manipulate you or fundamentally transform how you respond to people and how you engage with them. You will recognize when people are trying to use your emotional states and trying to take advantage of you. You will also learn how to use these techniques in ethical ways so that you can guide people to take the best action for themselves or the action you think they should take. Beyond everything, you will discover through the dark psychology what exactly is triggering your behaviors and, in part two, how to change those triggers if they are not going to be helpful or serve you in the way that you want them to.

Dark Psychology involves the use of mind tricks, which is in between deception and persuasion. The psychological mind tricks might sound outrageous, but it works well. They are being used to mislead people to think that what they know to be right is wrong, and what they believe to be wrong is right.

In a simple term, dark psychology allows humans to be willing and deliberate to harm others through their decisions and actions; sometimes, this might not be physical. However, some emotions are groomed from a very early stage of an individual's life. For example, a child grows to learn how to cry so that the adults around will make themselves available for their bidding. We can call this crying a manipulative tool for the child to be enabled to control people around. As a child grows up, if such as a child is not being cautioned on what he's doing, the so-called innocent childish behavior would now become a dark way of controlling people to do what he/she wants.

Dark psychology is the study of how a person thinks and sees a need to understand the intent behind actions and words. In general, it illuminates the dark side of human nature. In dark psychology, the effect is experienced by both the victim and the perpetrator. The personality traits which are considered as dark include narcissism, psychopathy, and Machiavellianism.

In a simple term, an excessive admiration of oneself in an obsessive manner towards appearance is referred to as narcissism. Narcissists usually feel superior. They do not subscribe to the rule of giving and take in a normal relationship. They are good at blaming others whenever there is an issue. A common feature is to be an extremely self-centered individual. Narcissists have a public appetite for control and power. They control people by making them think that they are looking out for them. They are also very smart such that they get involved in your day to day activities in life without being noticed. Above all, they are Keen liars and master is the lie skills.

Psychopathy is a trait that is associated with not being sensitive to other people. A psychopath will almost not have empathy for other people. Psychopaths are usually bold, confident, and fearless. They are risk-takers and extremely charming.

On the other hand, the third personality trait is known as Machiavelli's; the term is used to describe someone who lacks emotions and desire to achieve something at the expense of other people's feelings. This can be done through deceit, manipulation, or going against some moral rules. An individual who scores highly in Machiavelli's test is usually referred to as a "High Mach." These people are always around us, sometimes in our workplace or as a neighbor. They are hard-working people who are smart and are unapologetic about stepping on other people's toe. This set of people are opportunists and can emotionally detach themselves from situations they are in. Due to this ability, they are capable of involving themselves in several sexual several encounters. They can stand a chance of being good teammates but certainly not a good friend.

This knowledge of dark psychology is to protect yourself from those personalities when you come across them. Dark psychology cuts across all human conditions in which are universal. It studies how the state of humans relates to their thoughts, feelings, and perception. The general assumption here is that every human has the potential to be violent. Learning this concept is of two-folded benefits. First, it helps individuals accept that they tend to become evil, so the knowledge of this will prevent it from erupting. And secondly, it gives everyone a reason to struggle to survive.

The following concept I will be talking about is Neuro-Linguistics Programming (NLP). This is a technique used in restructuring people's minds on how to get rid of bad habits, how to become productive, and how to make them effective in general. You can use this technique to connect sense, mind, behavior, and language. This method is designed so that you tend to control people without them even being aware of what you are doing to them.

Neuro refers to the nervous system, which is made up of the mind and all other senses. Your nervous system functions when you interact with your environment or people. That's why when you listen more to people, you get to understand what is being said. When you pay more attention to what happens around you, you know and see more things about people around you.

Chapter 2. Explication of Dark Psychology

S everal skills are essential in analyzing people. The first and perhaps most important skill is having an understanding of human nature and normal human behavior. If you do not understand how humans behave under normal circumstances or what motivates most people, you are unlikely to interpret others' actions and intentions correctly. Just as a judge relies on their sense of how people typically behave and what motivates them in their judgments, so too must you develop an understanding of the typical spectrum of human behavior to analyze someone properly.

Of course, human beings can behave in highly original ways, making analyzing them difficult at times. Although human beings frequently behave in typically human ways—like being jealous of others' success or envious of a colleague who just married a beautiful wife—sometimes people can surprise you. Indeed, some people never feel jealous or envious of others. Most poor people do not steal even though they may need this because it is not part of their character. Frequently the most significant, most flamboyant thief is the person who already has all that they need.

To analyze people, you are going to have to start with knowing how humans are generally. It includes understanding the spectrum of human emotion, the behaviors linked to these emotions, and the things that motivate people to do this. Everyone wears a mask, which means that sometimes the intentions of others are not always clear. But even with this mask, people can reveal their emotional state to you, the things that make them happy, and the things that make them sad.

We all wear a mask, but perhaps only FBI agents are so skilled that they never give you some clue. A spontaneous laugh, a twinkle in the eye, a giddy tapping of the foot: These are unconscious signs that men and women give of how they feel. Analyzing men and women will require understanding human behavior and interpreting what people say and do.

Non-Verbal Communication

Non-verbal communication refers to the little clues that others give us that convey essential information outside of language. Human beings are social animals, meaning we evolved in settings where we were generally close to one another rather than alone. For this reason, we developed the ability to perceive and interpret the signals that others send to indicate their emotional state, thoughts, and motivations.

It is easy to pay attention to words when we are attempting to analyze others. Still, because language is not always an accurate indication of how people feel, it is essential to pay attention to the non-verbal cues others send. These cues can include facial expression, body distance, and the position of hands, quick movements of the hands or the feet, and the like. These non-verbal cues are not specific to human beings. Non-human primates are excellent examples of how animal societies can be built without speech. From bearing of teeth to the tail position, apes have a language comprised entirely of non-verbal cues.

Differentiating Fake From Real Emotion

Analyzing others will require developing the ability to distinguish exact sentiment from a false one. Human beings know that others observe and interpret them, at least the intelligent ones do, so they have become adept at hiding their feelings. A typical example of this is someone who smiles even though they are not happy. Still, this hiding of emotion can mean angry when one is hurt or vulnerable. Human beings wear masks to protect themselves, as you must if you plan on defending yourself from practitioners of dark psychology. But protecting yourself also means analyzing people appropriately, and this means determining which emotions are real and which are not.

The practitioner of dark psychological tactics perceives you as prey, so they pay very close attention to your words, actions, and non-verbal cues: virtually anything that indicates what's going on inside. You may put a wall to make your emotions more difficult for the predator to access, but you will most likely say or do something to reveal the truth. This is just as true of the predator as it is of you, the prey. They can put on a façade of smiles and pleasantries, but sometimes all it takes is one fierce look to reveal that their intentions are not so friendly.

We see this all the time in films and television shows. The new neighbor seems nice, but the camera shot reveals their subtle change in expression when your back is turned. They are not so neighborly. Their goal is to steal your husband and wreak havoc in your life (in the case of the standard Lifetime Original Movie). To protect yourself, you need to use your understanding of human nature and analyze it to figure out what is going on. Is there a discrepancy between the surface emotion and the events taking place? Perhaps the other person is smiling, but you heard that they lost their house and are short of funds. Would most people be so giddy in this situation?

An essential part of distinguishing real from fake emotion is deciding whether the surface or "fake" feeling makes sense, given what you know. Human beings are good at being emotionally aware by dint of being so communal. A person can hide what they feel, but it may only take a brief glimmer of real emotion for you to establish the rule of what is real in this person and what is not. The other person drops their mask for a second and notes what the natural person beneath looks like.

Tips to Identify a Liar

Anyone who has spent time around a pathological liar knows that little tricks can be used to tell when fibbing. Pathological liars are often highly friendly people who love to talk and always have something to say. It is this still having something to say that gets them into trouble. If you are suspicious that the person you are speaking to is a pathological liar, pay attention to the factual aspects of the things they say. This will become natural in time as you become aware the person is lying. You will make a mental note about facts like a specific monetary amount of something, a date, or a restaurant's name because you know these things may potentially be false.

Paying close attention to the details is the first step in identifying a liar. The second is knowing when to face the liar with the facts. It may not be a good idea to confront them pointedly, as you may decide. If they said they went to a particular restaurant, ask them what they had to eat—baked chicken and mixed vegetable stir fry. The next day, s/he asks them how the steak was. If they say, it was beautiful when you have caught them. They did not go to the restaurant at all. A pathological liar tells so many lies that they cannot keep track of them.

Chapter 3. How To Use Dark Psychology

How Can Psychology Improve Your Life?

T he following are some of the top ten realistic uses for psychology in regular life:

1. Get Prompted

Whether your purpose is to stop smoking, lose weight, or examine a new language, psychology training provides pointers for buying motivation. To grow your motivation while drawing close to a project, make use of some of the following tips derived from research in cognitive and educational psychology:

- Introduce new or novel factors to hold your interest high.

- Vary the series to help stave off boredom.

- Study new matters that build on your present understanding.

- Set clear goals that might be at once related to the assignment.

2. Enhance Your Management Abilities

It doesn't count number in case you're an office supervisor or a volunteer at a neighborhood teenage activity group; having true leadership abilities will, in all likelihood, be vital sometime in the future for your existence. Now, not all of us are born leaders, but some easy suggestions from mental studies can improve your leadership capabilities.

One of the most famous research papers on this topic looked at three distinct management styles. Primarily based on the findings of this look at and subsequent studies, practice several of the following when you are in a management function:

- Offer clear steering but permit group contributors to voice opinions.

- Communicate approximately possible answers to troubles with contributors to the group.

- Focus on stimulating ideas and be inclined to praise creativity.

3. Come to be a Better Communicator

Conversation involves a whole lot more than just the way you speak or write. Research indicates that nonverbal indicators make up a big portion of our interpersonal communications

Some key strategies encompass the subsequent:

- Use proper eye contact.

- Start noticing nonverbal indicators in others.

- Learn to use your tone of voice to boost your message.

4. Learn To Better Understand Others

Just like nonverbal communication, your capacity to apprehend your emotions and the feelings of those around you perform an important role in your relationships and professional lifestyles. The time emotional intelligence refers to your potential to apprehend each of your emotions in addition to those of other human beings.

What can you do to emerge as more emotionally stable? Recall a few of the subsequent techniques:

- Cautiously assess your very own emotional reactions.

- Record your enjoyment and emotions in a journal.

- Try to see situations from the angle of a different person.

5. Make Extra Correct Selections

Studies in cognitive psychology supply a wealth of statistics about choice making. By making use of those techniques for your lifestyles, you can discover ways to make wiser choices. The following time you want to make a huge decision, strive the usage of several the subsequent techniques:

- Try using the "Six Thinking Hats" technique with the aid of searching on the situation from multiple points of view, including rational, emotional, intuitive, creative, advantageous, and Dark views.

- Recall the capacity prices and blessings of choice.

- Appoint a grid evaluation approach that offers a score for how a selected decision will fulfill unique requirements you may have.

6. Enhance Your Reminiscence

Have you ever wondered why you can remember the precise information of childhood events yet forget the call of the new customer you met yesterday? Research on how we form new reminiscences and how and why we forget has caused some of the findings that can be implemented without delay in your daily life.

What are some methods you can grow your reminiscence of electricity?

- Awareness of the data.

- Rehearse what you have discovered.

- Do away with distractions.

7. Make Wiser financial decisions

Nobel Prize-winning psychologist Daniel Kahneman and his colleague Amos Tversky performed a chain of research that looked at how humans manipulate uncertainty and danger while making decisions.

One looks at located that workers could extra than triple their financial savings by making use of some of the following strategies:

- Don't procrastinate. Start investing savings now.

- Commit earlier to dedicate quantities of your future profits to your retirement financial savings.

- Try to be aware of non-public biases that may result in Dark money choices.

8. Get Higher Grades

The subsequent time you are tempted to whine about pop quizzes, midterms, or finals, consider that research has confirmed that taking checks helps you better consider what you have learned, even if it wasn't on the test.

Every other study discovered that repeated check-taking might be a higher reminiscence aid than studying. College students who were tested repeatedly have been able to remember 61% of the content while looking at the group recalled the most effective 40%. How can you observe those findings to your lifestyles? While seeking to research new data, self-check frequently to cement what you have learned into your memory.

9. Become More Effective

Occasionally, it looks as if there are hundreds of books, blogs, and magazine articles telling us the way to get more completed in an afternoon. However, how much of this advice is based on real studies? For example, think about the variety of times you have ever heard that multitasking can help you become more productive. Studies have discovered that trying to carry out multiple missions at the same time severely impairs pace, accuracy, and productiveness.

What classes from psychology can you operate to boom your productivity? Consider several of the following:

- Avoid multitasking while running on complex or dangerous obligations.

- Cognizance at the venture at hand.

- Eliminate distractions.

10. Be Healthier

Psychology also can be a useful device for improving your ordinary health. From approaches to encourage workout and better nutrients to new remedies for melancholy, the sector of fitness psychology gives a wealth of beneficial strategies that can help you to be more healthy and happier.

Some examples that you may practice at once in your very own existence:

- Research has shown that both daylight and synthetic mild can reduce the symptoms of seasonal affective sickness.

- Studies have demonstrated that exercise can contribute to more mental well-being.

- Studies have determined that supporting people apprehend the dangers of bad behaviors can lead to healthier choices.

Chapter 4. Delving Into Dark Psychology

S ome of the best science fiction that has ever been written has surrounded the subject of mind control and its ability to control our world. However, it can still sound like a futuristic event. However, many neuroscientists are continuing to create a digital interface specifically designed to connect to the brain, which has continued to make progress in recent times. Even though this advanced technology is still unreachable, it has made plenty of headway where we could see mind control gadgets popping up everywhere shortly.

Currently, a technology known as brain-computer interfaces, or BCIs, has only been in the development stage for individuals who have fallen victim to injuries, debilitating such as being paralyzed. A great example of this is a paraplegic by the name of Dennis DeGray. Neuroscientists at Stanford University assisted DeGray in creating a major breakthrough and a typing world record involving mind control.

DeGray's success partially stems from the assistance of Jaimie Henderson. Henderson, a neurosurgeon at Stanford, successfully implanted two electrodes arrays the size of a tic-tac into DeGray's brain. DeGray's brain activity is then monitored by the electrode arrays, which helps decode electrical brain signals that neurons fire deep in the brain's motor cortex. The results achieved were beyond impressive and allowed for the early steps of achieving independence for many currently fully or partially paralyzed people. With a lot of interest pointed towards this ability to control the environment through a BCI, many researchers hope that future demonstrations can further the technology in the future ahead. It could even be as soon as the next 5-10 years that we could see more of it being integrated into people's lives.

Besides the research and development being conducted at Stanford, another company seems to be taking it one step further. Neural ink, founded by Tesla and SpaceX CEO Elon Musk, has become dedicated to creating BCI that they have labeled as "neural lace." To date, Neuralink has already raised close to $30 million for funding the project.

Nevertheless, like anything connected to the internet, one has to be extremely careful and diligent in the security and safe handling of all devices so that the device's security does not become compromised. We saw this occur when the Mirai botnet practically destroyed many internet areas that created attacks that used Denial of Service. Once a person's brain is implanted and connected to an internet device, this is when an entirely new level of security issues could occur, including a possible 'brain jacking.' Not only for security purposes, but it also could lead to many questions about ethical responsibility. For example, if a brain-controlled machine breaks the law, then who is arrested for it? Problems like this would need to require in-depth discussion before our future becomes a place where mind control is used for everything. However, in the short-term, an interface that is a less invasive brain-computer is already in use and which have significantly lower risks.

Many headsets have been developed and used in many drone races successfully as well as controlling Mind Desktop, which is a brain interface that is generalized for the use of Windows. With these devices, they bring less of a risk than implanting a chip into your brain. Not only that, but they do lack a few things too, especially with performance. This is seen with Mind Desktop, where a character is typed in 20 seconds. Regardless of that, they are still pretty cheap because of their use of electronics that have been modified. Therefore, if you currently have Mind Desktop, you are using an $800 "electroencephalogram" (a medical device used to measure brain activity) for a fraction of the real machine's cost.

When it comes to external BCI challenges, they mostly surround the skull, brain coverings, and scalps density and thickness. These characteristics prevent us from snooping on the brain's neurons with accuracy, which is what we think is essential for a BCI system to be high performing. As far as the future is concerned, we can only get remotely close to the information found on neurons is if we get an implant placed inside.

With many researchers making attempts to build a better BCI, other researchers have continued with their BCI implant technology. However, they have been experiencing technical issues of their own, which they will need to overcome. First, they hope to obtain an increased amount of views from their sensors, which will increase their ability to decode faster brain signals a lot more accurately. Plus, there remains the question of getting these outsides of the laboratory so people can use them.

These BCI's need to be constructed not to require a technician or some third-party intervention is of high importance since the main goal includes restoring people's independence while being paralyzed. This is why researchers are continuing to address these issues actively.

The erasing and implanting of memories seem to be only capable in movies such as Total Recall, Dark City, and Inception. But this idea no longer sounds as farfetched as we once thought since many people do not even lose sleep over the fact that it could happen someday. But now we can begin to see a brighter future with ontogenetic and how it continues to tamper with memory to bring it to light eventually. Although ontogenetic is still a relatively new procedure in the experimental stage, it has broken some laboratory ground. It uses light to activate or inactivate neurons that are highly specific by way of light-sensitive channels. For these to be used, they also require sensitive proteins. A few of these proteins include halorhodopsin or channelrhodopsin, which are added to the subject. These proteins are found naturally in many organisms. They need to be inserted genetically into an organism like in a rat or mice in the laboratory. Once injected, the neuron will fire every time the light is activated. When the light is on, the light enacts discretionary particles' progression, such as calcium or sodium, making the neuron produce an activity potential.

This system has been utilized in mice to control their eating or drinking propensities. The mice are hereditarily built to have these light-touchy proteins, and a wire is embedded into their cerebrum. Specialists demonstrated that the mice would keep eating while the light is turned on, regardless of whether they do not feel hungry. The best way to prevent the mice from eating is by killing the light. By basically turning on or off a light, one can control a neuron from terminating, bringing about certain and automatic conduct changes. This procedure can be utilized to figure out which neurons are required for specific activities. Likewise, researchers would now be able to figure out what capacity a neuron has by initiating it or deactivating and watching the impacts.

There have been a few speculations that caffeine may avert memory deficiencies by restraining the adenosine A2A receptor. A recent report demonstrated that the actuation of adenosine A2A receptor in the hippocampus, utilizing ontogenetic, was sufficient to weaken spatial memory in mice. This investigation not just exhibits the relationship between caffeine and abatement

27

in memory misfortune; however, this additionally demonstrates the likelihood of erasing and hindering recollections in mice utilizing ontogenetic. Another investigation demonstrated that if neurons in the thalamic core reunions were initiated utilizing ontogenetic, the working memory in mice indicated deficiencies. As this system turns out to be further developed and used, researchers will frequently have a superior comprehension of which neurons influence memory and how they influence it.

Ontogenetic was utilized to take a gander at the impact of core cucumbers (NAC) on the "cocaine-setting related" memory guideline. They found that when the NAC neurons were enacted, the mice basically "overlooked" that cocaine was situated in that district. The researcher likewise saw that the actuation caused a diminished number of c-Fos+ cells in the VP, which has recently been related to a "decline in medication chasing." They presumed that these neurons were significant for the directing prize looking for conduct brought about by cocaine. This might be significant for deciding how a habit is shaped and maybe helping expansion issues.

This demonstrates the significance of certain natural triggers for medication addicts. If ontogenetic can help cancel the recollections engaged with the situations, it can have exceptional consequences for how we treat chronic drug habits. Not exclusively would memories be able to be deleted, yet false recollections can likewise be included. A recent report demonstrated that when dentate gyrus neurons were enacted, mice solidified in a spot where they had never been stunned, indicating dread. This dread was not there earlier, yet after the light was demonstrated, these mice had recollections of dread in a novel spot.

Even though ontogenetic is genuinely new, it is rapidly being consolidated into numerous tests. It is enabling us to all the more likely comprehend what impact enacting or deactivating neurons has on conduct. Unmistakably it is conceivable, at any rate in mice, to cause a mouse to do certain things utilizing optogenetics; we can even eradicate recollections and "make" new ones. One day those science fiction films may not look so inconceivable.

I do not mean the enthusiastic control intentionally used to get our particular manner. I mean the capacity to get others to figure out how we do and concur with us, just by the sheer quality of psyche.

Consider despots who can bewilder hordes of individuals with quality of speech while on the ascent to control. Analyze the content sometime in the not too distant future. You think it is difficult to see in what capacity numerous individuals moved toward becoming influenced around then. Consider a well-prepared canine or horse and the association with their proprietor. A steed is more grounded than the proprietor, and a canine normally increasingly deft, yet they obey directions. Consider the impact of "charm." How does a specific entertainer hold a crowd of people while similar words or activities by another entertainer are less captivating?

Are these things the aftereffect of the idea structure billows of extraordinary power, created by a solitary individual who empties their feelings into the conveyance and into that idea structure cloud? Rather than a few contemplations, social events to cause a solid cloud can include a solitary individual who has excellent conviction and self-conviction blended with crude feeling produce their cloud that overwhelms the psyches in the crowd?

In most close to home connections, there are fluctuating degrees of control, some favoring one individual one minute and the other the following minute. Equalization is accomplished at the point when intense feeling bolsters amazing personalities.

Chapter 5. The History of Dark Psychology

Human mythology is riddled with tales of ghosts and creatures that behave in such drastic ways. The very description sends chills down the adults' length that listened to such stories as relayed by past musicians and bards. The creation of monsters advises us that perhaps the universe is not as secure as it might seem from within our window. Beasts live among us and render our lifestyles as something to be protected against, as anything to be covered.

Maybe a creature crawls out of the closet while you rest in your room or slips in from a backdoor that you failed to lock. Perhaps you assumed you were over there, but as it enters your door, you listen to footprints crackling upstairs and a soft voice roaring. You see a bushy, tail-like foot poking out beneath the bed or a claw. You notice a massive, vicious laugh while running for life. You sprint into the shower, and the door is locked. It's not necessarily a stellar exit strategy as there is no window in your toilet, but you didn't know where to get off. Maybe the beast is on the escalators. You don't know where everything is. But after that, you push the above head bathroom light chain and see that you are the monster.

Monsters exist among humans and are medically related to as H. Sapiens... sapiens. Aliens from some other world did not commit actions of murder, theft, and ruin. They were living things who decided to commit these crimes, and today they also live among us. There is indeed a term in behavioral genetics, the so-called dark chord. Applies to the three characteristics of psychopathy, narcissism, and sociopathy, such as factors are deemed especially harmful, so distinguishing such people from the general public is necessary, or would it be?

Since ancient times, an argument could be made that human beings accept their character's horrific components. Today we believe in everyday practices of ancient history, such as orgiastic religious practices, human sacrifice, and ritualized murder as brutal acts of the past that indicate a better forgotten time. Still, it has been argued that these acts represent social and cultural outlets for the black universe that lies beneath the beautiful surface of the human outside.

Societies were then explicitly organized. This would be up upon you to determine whether things are more comfortable today or bad. As tacky as the past, as mentioned earlier, practices may have been, their career status within their living area represented an acknowledgment. That human being had a wrong side to their personality. It was great to give outlets to this dark side than to let it explode and simmer in unexpected ways. For what do today's gang stalking, serial murder, cybercrime, and narcissistic and antisocial acts portray, but living things give in to ends of themselves because they have already expressed themselves in other ways?

The argument is not to assert that living things must consider to give in to their so-called dark tendency of singularity, but to recommend that the contemporary art of mind control represents a variety of activities expressed in ancient society in unique ways. Although the conversation of societies' tradition of providing into their character's dark sides may seem incidental to the discussion of mind control, few things could be essential. A significant phase in planning for defense lies in understanding anyone, you know, maybe the perpetrator of these black arts. It could be someone you already understand.

History of Dark Psychology Study

The 2 social scientific patterns that proactive solutions-day dark psychology are undoubtedly abnormal psychology and psychology for individuals. Irregular psychology is a psychology experiment concerned with psychological illness-related habits of behaviors, emotion, and behavior. These emotions, thoughts, and actions can precede a psychiatric disorder and are usually thought abnormal. As psychology tends to construct a relatively linear dichotomy between normal versus strange behavior, a sociological factor will come under the scepter between irregular or atypical behavioral forms instead of actions assumed to be inside the usual spectrum.

In the early late nineteenth century, person psychology was founded on human conduct driven by the purposeful activity compared to latent libido and sex impulses that describe Freudian psychoanalysis. While we have already addressed in some depth the degree to which individual acts are not consciously driven. May thus be viewed as non-purpose, person psychology allows for implicit or involuntary motives. It just appears to recognize them when non-Freudian, benevolent, and even not always implicit.

For example, as a motivating factor for action, Alfred Adler focused many of his texts on superiority complexes. He found that people who handled the situation in angry or otherwise unbecoming ways were generally inspired by a sense of inadequacy, which is a certain sense caused them to "act out." Now in some people, an inferiority complex as an enthusiastic may lie beneath the surface. However, others may be fully aware that they have a feature of themselves. They are not completely satisfied and trying to compensate.

When creating dark psychology as an outgrowth of internal mental ideas compared to Freudian psychoanalysis concepts, it may be simpler to assume. That human beings usually act with conscious, deliberate motivations instead of being consciously or unconsciously inspired by sexual urges, such as the well-studied complex of Oedipus (the desire for a man to kill his father and sleep). To truly comprehend the historical growth of dark psychology as a research field, it is crucial to realize that individual psychology's philosophy requires non-completely aware motives to explain why human beings tend to act in such a cruel fashion. Even so, the theory of dark psychology supposes that humans are capable of a dark universe, engaging in harmful actions that have no purpose at all.

The research and therapy of psychological disorders have been around as a field of study since the Ancient Egyptians. We have more data from the Greek period, partly because we are closer to the Greek philosophy period in time than we are from the Egyptians. This group just seems to reach the concept of pathology with a fascinating avidity. The research of what we term pathological psychology today existed in the 18th and 19th centuries and earlier in asylum and hospices that diagnosed people and women with rare mental disorders, but the discipline as we now know it dates from the 20th century.

Indeed, in the 19th century, trepanation, exorcism, and being burnt on the stakes as a witch were the standard remedies for pathological mental conditions. Trepanation relates to drilling a hole in the brain to expel malignant spirits from their grip over the head. It is claimed by others to be the earliest surgical technique we have historical evidence. Trepanation was already performed in the 19th century. Today, there are proponents of the procedure, though their appeals usually fell on deaf ears.

Exorcism also looks at how society viewed odd habits and emotions in the current age. Indeed, many practices that we consider to fall inside the normal range today have been considered mental diseases up till the early 1980s. Exorcism, although maybe less brutal than trepanation, represented the perspective that an evil force or demon inhabited the individual who possessed the weird thoughts and actions. All this has been a transmission from the individual's malevolent encouragement to anything else, whether something else was an informant of evil or an agent of evil.

One line of thinking recognizes Satan as the manifestation of human potential to act in a manner "strange" or, more accurately, evil or cruel. It is hard to say whether their ideas of ghouls, demons, values, or even of Satan himself embody that people beings were produced to commit acts of possession. They could be better described as stories intended to fool children or teach them valuable life lessons of good and evil. Of course, exorcisms are still happening today; individuals who assume evil acts come from ownership.

If you believe that the evil committed by human beings comes from a source outside the human being, then the dark psychological theory because it currently stands may be somewhat contrary to what you believe. However, a locally crucial in dark psychology is the idea that humans can behave without purpose in a remarkably violent and cruel manner, only as an augmentation of something obscure that dwells inside us. It is up to you to ascribe this type of conduct to Satan as a component of your religious views.

Of course, 19th-century and later abnormal psychologists did not fully recognize this idea of an independent factor for the conditions they were seeing. So treatments such as trepanation or exorcism would've been disturbing or at least pointless to them. As we commented on earlier, scientists shifted away towards the dogmatic beliefs that dominated their careers, ideologies that mostly had more to do with theology than with the professions' empirical compendia. There is nothing intrinsically inconsistent with religious belief, of course. Still, a practitioner who is inexperienced with human anatomy if he is not permitted to examine q cadaver is probably to follow a religion that is not advantageous to him (or herself) or you.

Abnormal psychologists started to question why humans were inspired to behave abnormally. The Devil or the Demons were not entirely acceptable responses. Most of these research groups in psychological disorders were psychiatrists and psychoanalysts who undertook detailed studies of these subjects based on a new, more free understanding of health matters. Though the word dark psychology did not emerge until later in the mid-twentieth century, narcissists, sociopaths, and those who we might identify today as possessing mental illnesses were conducted already throughout the 19th-century studies.

Abnormal psychology of that time would have followed the trend of what we now understand as Freudian psychoanalysis, with Alfred Adler's writings representing one of Freudian's first significant departures. Although Adler is a virtually unknown figure today, his biographies from the generations 1912-1914 provided the basis of many concepts that permeate today's psychological field. His writings were translated into English in 1925. And his personality beliefs and where they derive from predominate in advance psychotherapy and psychoanalysis.

Adler focused on resignation, compensation, and over-compensation as the 3 external factors that shaped personality development. His theories parallel those of another essential psychologist, Abraham Maslow, who acknowledged Alder's influence on his work. Although Adler himself didn't even write about "dark psychology," his theories helped shape this topic's development as a departure from pre-existing psychoanalytical theories.

The analysis of dark psychology can be new. Still, it reflects a spectrum of habits that have been associated with individuals from the very start. The dark area of psychology provides the illusion of a transient research domain. The word and the principles connected with it are more widely available to the people. This has turned dark psychological into a topic that remains beyond the radar of those who may be victims of perpetrators exploiting their resources to damage impact.

Chapter 6. Advanced Techniques to Manipulate Human Psychology

S ources tell us that it is concealment—hiding in the shadows, knowing when to strike. It is also a false front, hiding true intentions. When we are talking about this level of deception, we are talking about hiding aggression. When we take, there is a certain level of aggressive behavior that happens. A small part of manipulation is hiding that aggressive behavior so that the victim sees only good nature.

This is accomplished in various ways and means, one being knowledge. When we allow another to know us, we display vulnerability along with strengths. The experience of these personality traits can give the manipulator the ability to maneuver around without any alarms going off.

- The effectiveness of manipulating those strengths and vulnerabilities arrives when the dark practitioner knows what is vulnerable and inspires pride.

A reoccurring ideology that drives us to war takes into consideration that the action is more negative than positive. We want to avoid it. The manipulation process sees pride in all of us and plays to that pride. It is our strength. For example, when used to drive an army to slaughter others, the intention of our satisfaction has been manipulated to enforce the agendas of others.

- Often, the practitioners of dark psychology use aggression and fear to drive us. The less dark side still falls into the category of knowing what weakness is. That weakness leaves the individual open to control.

How the manipulator uses that control determines the severity of manipulation. There are positive versions of manipulating others, like convincing someone that they are not doing well and needing help. We, however, are looking at the darker side of this. The manipulator uses their control skills to get what they want—and the cost does not apply.

- There are many ways to move another into a place of being controlled. From the positive to the negative, psychological manipulators utilize all tactics.

When positive reinforcement is used, the charm is displayed. A forced smile or laughter can trigger laughter in all of us. As when we were infants, we copy what we see. When we see tears, we want them to stop. When we see a smile, we find ourselves smiling as well. Using positive reinforcement, the manipulator can shower money, charm, and gifts to get us to feel something. The usage of these things allows control of us on an instinctual level. We follow those who tell us what we want to hear.

- Psychological manipulation can also implement negative reinforcement. This is a form of deflection—the substitution of one thing for another.

Often, we have things we need or have to do, and we do not want to do them. The psychological manipulation of negative reinforcement uses that power of negativity to lure the subject from their original need, pushing them toward something they want to be done instead. The long game, a slow play of putting tasks into another's life and then controlling those tasks so that the manipulator can get what they want, is an extraordinarily useful and subdued tactic. Sometimes only partial reinforcement is required to gain control. We are talking about elevating the fear or doubt regarding the tasks needed to be done. The partial is the extended play. It knows that in the end, the victim will lose. It knows that by planting small seeds now, victory will eventually happen. It knows that we all have our weaknesses and that by planting even a tiny seed, we can take someone to that weakness. An individual trying to work toward something they already were shaky on or had doubts about will listen to the lie and flow with that idea, and use it to their destruction.

- The partial manipulator only needs to put the thought in mind, knowing the weakness is already there, and utilizing it will take their prey to a destructive end.

Psychological manipulators flat, outright punish. From an actual physical lashing to the victim's passive-aggressive playing, punishment is beneficial when one wants to control another.

- We skulk and cry and yell and nag and go completely silent. This is the blackmail of the manipulator. It inspires guilt in us. That "wanting to be the better person" rises to the front, and we do what the manipulator wants. When the manipulator sets free the crocodile tears, we have no idea if they are real or not. The degree of crying is not up to us to determine. Only the manipulator knows if the tears are legitimate or not. In this case, the trap is often sprung from the victim's side. They walk up to the hurt individual to help, only to find that the manipulator is just lying in wait to strike.

- One extreme version of manipulation is violence.

Violence triggers something inside us. We often do anything to avoid it. The manipulator knows that power strategically applied can make us go into a state of avoidance. There incites the control, physical violence can have mental scarring, and the manipulator causes the scarring. It places power in tactical places to get the result they want.

Some would say this is the darkest of the dark. Taken to the individual, this can mentally damage them for an extended period, if not permanently. Placed on a world stage, it can lead up to the physical conflict of genocide.

• Mostly, it is about gain. Manipulators of the dark want to gain something. When we speak about improvement, we are talking about power and influence, control and manipulation over others. The trophy is up to the individual. This can be everything as to gaining affections, to money, and even to life itself.

It is about gaining for their reasons and gratifications. The taking of others and making the power and control their own. Selfishness to the extreme. The mind of the dark practitioner sees the ultimate win as the gain over others. They have power. Superiority is the power over another, and taking of someone else's power makes them feel superior. This is a tremendous driving force behind the manipulator. Often, in the case of immature individuals driving manipulations toward superiority, any is pushed aside for just the feeling of being superior. In relationships, it is about control. The manipulation of power can put one in control. Although we have looked at the vampire and energy role, we know who has control.

This feeling of control can be overwhelming to the mental state of the dark. Almost drug-like, it is a feeling of emotion that is more logical. Management is one of the most straightforward manipulation tactics to achieve with only logic to guide. It drives not only the victim but the manipulator as well. Psychological manipulation can also be about self-esteem. The self of the manipulator is always in question. This is one of the reasons they manipulate, to define themselves. How easily they can manage, another can tell the dark that they are better than others. That weakness and strength can be measured in the tactical playing field of the hustle.

- The dark psychological manipulator is bored most of the time, more than most. The psychological manipulator will often use manipulation to determine the validity of feelings and emotions.

This boils down to that manipulation applied in relations with others helps the manipulator regulate reactions to validate or not validate their own emotions. The manipulator measures the self and their self-esteem by how others handle their self-questioning. This happens when the practitioner does not have a grasp on what emotions are. They look at their feelings as invalid and manipulate the situation in such a way as to validate them. We are stuck with ourselves, and we cannot get away. Psychological manipulators validate or invalidate themselves by the tactical controlling of others. It is an exciting way of viewing life, although we all idolize one form of manipulation.

- **The con aspect.** One common form of manipulation is the convincing of another to make their money's yours. This is a hidden agenda of the criminal. This form of mental manipulation preys mostly on the elderly and the rich. However, we all can fall into this form of manipulation. We choose to spend on, and we do not respond to a state of psychological manipulation.

Something happens when the buck is passed over, we go from manipulation into action, and something drives us. It is within us, and it is outside forces that drive. What causes this drive and the drive itself is called Persuasion.

The manipulation process in dark psychology usually is not a single move. It is a complex series of actions, often with the outcome only known by the manipulator. The motivations of manipulators are as convoluted as human nature.

Chapter 7. Mind Control

M ind control is an aspect of manipulation that is similar to brainwashing. The main difference is that the individual might only want to control your mind at the moment. Maybe they want to get you to do something that will benefit them temporarily because they are opportunistic individuals. Since there is not much time to take over a person's mind when you are engaged in a simple conversation, there are some very detailed techniques that a manipulator will use to attempt to gain control of your mind. As you explore these techniques, you will also learn how to combat each of them. The stronger your reason is, the better you will ward off the people trying to harm you.

Compensating for Lack of Physical Prowess

Someone might try to control your mind because you secretly intimate them. Because someone does not appear physically threatening, a manipulator will be quick to move forward with mind control by seeing how much they can change your thoughts. The mind control gives them the same type of satisfaction they would receive if they were physically controlling you. Because the latter is a lot more prominent, the idea of controlling your mind is also a lot more appealing. You will find that manipulators are very discreet about this.

They might remark on how strong or tough you are, building you up based on your physical characteristics. Even a simple comment about you being tall can be enough to let you think that they respect you because you have more physical prowess than they do—this is what they want you to think. Instead of backing down, which you will think they are doing, they make you more vulnerable by making you comfortable.

When you believe that someone sees powerful traits in you, you will be less likely to assume that they have bad intentions. Surely because they appear to respect you, they won't deceive you, right? Always make sure that you remind yourself anyone can fool you at any time. It is hard to keep track of everyone's true intentions, especially when they have mastered the art of mind control.

What You Can Do: Remain firm in your core beliefs. Even if you believe that the individual respects you and what you stand for, always remind yourself of what you hold dear to your heart. Staying true to who you give you little reason to change your opinions on a whim. Remind yourself that the person trying to control your mind is very insecure.

Using Hand Placement as a Decoy

Have you ever noticed that people normally place their fingers on their heads when thinking very hard? In moments of concentration, you have probably done the same thing. This is a subconscious mind control technique that is often used by manipulators. When they want you to rethink something, they might place their fingers on their head to coax you into doing the same. With the help of muscle memory, your brain will be receiving a message that it needs to think harder.

It is an interesting technique because it is so subtle. You surely would not notice it if you were not looking for it in the first place. As you become better at reading body language, you will become more aware of moments when the person you are talking to is merely using a decoy movement as an attempt to control you. Do your best to break the mirroring effect that typically happens during a conversation. Keep your arms in a neutral position by your side.

Manipulators get nervous. They probably get very nervous and will do the best they can to hide this from you. As soon as you notice their fingers move up to their head, imagine that they are nervous that they won't be able to pull off this attempt at mind control. Pride yourself in your ability to pick up on it before it affects you—this will keep you strong.

What You Can Do: In an attempt to break their cycle, you can make a comment that indirectly refers to them concentrating. Something like, "Oh, is that what you were thinking?" is a way to make manipulators second-guess their abilities. If you let them know from the start that you are not automatically going to agree with what they are saying, this will be your way of standing your ground.

Convincing You of Psychic Powers

The person who is manipulating you is not any more powerful than you—repeat this to yourself often. Even though many mind controllers are portrayed as psychic beings, this is not the case for most. A successful manipulator is usually just very good at picking up on your body language and context. There is nothing psychic about it, though it can feel that way at times.

Being misinformed that someone is psychic and can read your mind at any time is intimidating. These are your private thoughts, and you do not want anyone intruding upon them. The good news is that you never have to let this happen. You are still in control of your inner thoughts, and what you share with the world is always going to be your decision. Anyone who tries to force you or to coax you into sharing something you do not want to does not have your best interest at heart.

45

The mention of psychic abilities might come up as a joke. For example, the manipulator will joke around with you while mentioning that you don't need to say much because they already know what you are thinking. You can laugh this off, but you can also remain firm in believing that this isn't true. With the way you portray yourself, you can get them to think anything you want.

What You Can Do: Always be aware of your intention during every conversation. If you are presenting yourself in a certain way, the manipulative person will pick up on it. Try your hardest to practice standing neutrally and speaking neutrally. When you can master this concept, it will be a lot harder for them to read you.

Surrounding You with Other Manipulative People

This is an incredibly dangerous mind-control technique because it closely ties in with the idea behind brainwashing. The more people that you believe are on the same page about something will make you want to agree with them, too. If a manipulator can find other people who want to manipulate a vulnerable person, you might become an easy target for a bad situation. They will gang up on you in a way that is subtle yet effective. You do not have to put up with this. Knowing who you are as a person will protect you in many ways.

There will be times when a manipulator will only "scout" for like-minded individuals that believe in the point they are making. Unknowingly, they might recruit innocent bystanders to further lead you into thinking that you must agree with them. The people that also fall victim to these traps might be people you love and respect. This is why it might be tempting to give in and to just "go with the flow." It is what the manipulator wants you to think. They want others to know that it is easier to go with a mass opinion than form their own.

What You Can Do: Speak up when you disagree with something. This is difficult because you do not want to cause conflict or controversy, but it becomes necessary to protect yourself. A disagreement does not always have to turn into an argument. If you approach the situation maturely, you can simply speak your mind to get your point across without requiring validation. You can provide this for yourself. Remind yourself that it is not other people's opinions that matter most. Your view of yourself dictates your self-esteem.

Believing it Won't Happen to You

Because a mind controller works hard to use other people, you might assume that they would instead do this to strangers or bystanders. One of the most challenging realities to face is that these individuals are more likely to attempt the act of mind control on a loved one. This happens because the task seems a lot easier—they already know you well. Instead of having to figure out the things that get under your skin, they have an idea of what to say and how to persuade you. Realizing this can be very hurtful, especially when you have many trusts invested in the person.

"I would never do anything to hurt you" is a promise that is often broken by a manipulator. With mind control, they are directly going against that promise, even if it doesn't feel hurtful at the moment. When someone does not respect you for who you are, they will do anything to change you. Suggesting you should get something else to eat or that you should shop elsewhere for clothing are two simple examples of how manipulators can use their conviction to change you.

You might not believe that these little changes mean much, but when you add them up, they can completely transform who you are as a person. It is not a great feeling to realize that you no longer recognize who you are. As upsetting as it is, you have to work on rebuilding yourself and getting back to your roots. It is normal to feel betrayed because this is what the manipulator has done to you—betrayed your trust.

What You Can Do: Never let your naive thinking get in the way of your rational thinking. You are not immune to the mind control that goes on around you. Your strength does not necessarily protect you from the intentions of all manipulators. By keeping yourself humble, you will always be on alert for the red flags presented by those who wish to change your mind.

The Blank Stares of Intimidation

Making a statement to someone and receiving a blank stare in return is intimidating for many reasons. One of the most prominent is that you do not know what they are thinking. It scares you because you might not know what to say or do next. A manipulator will use this technique to control your mind after you have said something vulnerable or profound. This will make you second-guess if what you said was "wrong" or incorrect somehow. You will end up prioritizing their feelings over your own.

They might follow this instance up with a statement that seems wise or all-knowing. When you combine the two actions, you are sure to believe that they can read your mind or that they know something you don't know. Both possibilities are unsettling in their ways. When you feel a negative emotion, understand that this is what your manipulator wants you to feel. They want to catch you off-guard and make you question everything that you have confirmed in your reality. By slowly breaking you down and staring at you blankly, you will get the idea that you came to this conclusion independently. It becomes maddening when you do not realize what is happening to you.

Chapter 8. Mind Control Techniques

M ind control involves using influence and persuasion to change the behaviors and beliefs of someone. That someone might be the person themselves, or it might be someone else. Mind control has also been referred to as brainwashing, thought reform, coercive persuasion, mental control, and manipulation, just to name a few. Some people feel that everything is done by manipulation. But if that is true to be believed, then important points about manipulation will be lost. Influence is much better thought of as a mental continuum with two extremes. One side has respectful and ethical influences and works to improve the individual while showing respect for them and their basic human rights. The other side contains dark and destructive influences that work to remove that human rights from a person, such as independence, rational thought, and sometimes their real identity.

When thinking of mind control, it is better to see it use influence on other people to disrupt something in them, as their way of thinking or living. The influence works based on what makes people human, such as their behaviors, beliefs, and values. It can disrupt the very way they chose personal preferences or make critical decisions. Mind control is nothing more than using words and ideas to convince someone to say or do something they might never have thought of saying or doing on their own.

There are scientifically proven methods that can be used to influence other people. Mind control has nothing to do with fakery, ancient arts, or even magical powers. Real mind control is the basis of a word that many people hate to hear. That word is marketing. Many people hate to hear that word because of the negative connotations associated with it. When people hear "marketing," they automatically assume that it refers to those ideas taught in business school. But the basis of marketing is not about deciding which part of the market to target or deciding which customers will likely buy this product. The basis of marketing is one very simple word. That word is "YES."

If a salesperson asks a regular customer to write a brief endorsement of the product they buy, they will hopefully say yes. If someone asks their significant other to take some of the business cards to pass out at work, they will hopefully say yes. If you write any blog and ask another blogger to provide a link to yours on their blog, they will hopefully say yes. When enough people say yes, the business or blog will begin to grow. With even more yesses, it will continue to grow and thrive. This is the very simple basis of marketing. Marketing is nothing more than using mind control to get other people to buy something or do something beneficial. And the techniques can easily be learned.

The first technique in mind control is to tell people what you want them to want. Never tell people to think it over or take some time. That is a definite mind control killer. People already have too much going on in their minds. When they are told to think something over, they will not. It will be forgotten, and then it will never happen. This has nothing to do with being stupid or lazy and everything to do with just being way too busy.

So the best strategy is to take the offensive and think for them. Everything must be explained in the beginning. Never assume that the other blogger will automatically understand the benefits of adding a link will be for them. Do not expect anyone to give a demonstration blindly. And merely asking for a testimonial, while it might garner an appositive response, probably will not garner a well-formed testimonial to the product. Instead, be prepared to explain the blog, show examples, and offer compelling reasons why this merger will benefit both parties. Have the demonstration laid out in great detail with notes on what to say when and visuals to go along with the letters, so all the other person has to do is present the information. Offer the customer a few testimonials that have already been received and ask them to choose one and personalize it a bit. Always be specific in explaining what is desired. Explain why it is desired. Show how this will work. Tell the person how to do it and why they should do it. If done correctly, it will feel exactly like one friend advising another friend on which is the best path to take. And the answer will be yes, simply because saying yes makes so much sense.

Think of the avalanche. Think of climbing all the way to the top of the highest mountain ever. Now, at the top, think of searching for the biggest, heaviest boulder on the mountain. Now, picture summoning up superhuman strength to push this boulder, dislodging it from the place it has rested for years and years. Once this boulder is loosened, it rolls easily over the edge of the cliff, crashing into thousands of other boulders on its way down the mountain, taking half of the mountain with it in a beautiful cascade of rocks and dirt. Imagine sitting there, smiling cheerfully at the avalanche that was just created.

Marketing and mind control are very like creating an avalanche. Getting the first person to answer yes might be difficult. But each subsequent yes will be easier. Always start at the top, never the bottom. Starting at the top is more complicated. It is more likely to come with more negative responses than positive responses in the beginning. But starting at the top also yields a much greater reward when the avalanche does begin. And the results will be far greater than beginning at the bottom of the mountain. Yes, the small rock is easier to push over. Then it can be built upon by pushing over another small rock, then another. This way can work, but it will take much longer than being successful at the top. No one ever went fishing for the smallest fish in the pond or auditioned for the secondary role just to be safe. Everyone wants that top prize. Do not be afraid to go for it.

On the other hand, never ask for the whole boulder the first time. Ask for part of it. This may seem directly contradictory, but it is not. Always start with a small piece. Make the beginning easier for everyone to see. Let other people use their insight to see the result. When the first bit goes well, then gradually ask for more and more and more.

Think of writing a guest spot for someone else who has their own blog. By sending in the entire manuscript first, there is a greater risk of rejection. Begin small. Send them a paragraph or two discussing them with the idea. Then outline the idea and send that in an email. Then write the complete draft you would like them to use and send it along. When asking a customer for a testimonial, start by asking for a few lines in an email. Then ask the customer to expand those few lines into a testimonial covering at least half a typed page. The customer will soon be ready for an hour-long webcast extolling the product's virtues and your great customer service skills.

Everything must have a deadline that exists. The important word here is the word 'real.' Everyone has heard the salesperson who said to decide right away because the deal might not be available later or another customer was coming in, and they might get it. That is a total fabrication, and everyone knows it to be true. There are no impending other customers, and the deal is not going to disappear. There is no real sense of urgency involved. But everyone does it. There are too many situations where people are given a fake deadline by someone who thinks it will instill a great sense of urgency for completing the task. It is not only totally not effective but completely unneeded. It is a simple matter to create true urgency. Only leave free things available for a finite amount of time. When asking customers for testimonials, be certain to mention the last possible day for it to be received to be able to be used. Some people will be unable to assist, but having people unable to participate is better than never beginning.

Always give before you receive it. And do not ever think that giving is fifty-fifty. Always give much more than is expected in return. Before asking for a testimonial from a satisfied customer, be sure to make numerous acts of exceptional customer service. Before asking a blog writer for a link, link theirs to yours many times. This is not about helping someone out so that they will help you. This is all about being so totally generous that the person who is asked for the favor cannot possibly say no. It might mean extra work, but that is how to influence other people.

Always stand up for something much bigger than average. Do not just write another blog on how to do something. Use a critical issue to take a stand and defend the stance with unbeatable logic and genuine passion. Do not just write a how-to manual. Choose a particular idea and sell people on it, using examples of other people with the same idea living the philosophy.

Never feel shame. This does not mean being extremely extroverted to the point of silliness or having a total lack of conscience in business dealings. In mind control, shamelessness refers to a full, complete belief that this course of action is the best possible course. Everyone will benefit greatly from it. This is about writing the best possible blog ever and believing that everyone needs to read it to improve their lives. It is about believing in a particular product so deeply that the feeling is that everyone will benefit from using it. Knowing deep inside that this belief is the correct belief ever and everyone should believe it.

Mind control uses the idea that someone's decisions and emotions can be controlled using psychological means. It uses negotiation or mental influence powers to ensure the outcome of the interaction is more favorable to one person over the other. This is what marketing is: convincing someone to do something particular or buy something in particular. Being able to control someone else's mind merely means understanding the power of human emotion and playing upon those emotions. It is easier to have a mental impact on people if there is a basic understanding of human emotions. Angry people will back down when the subject of their anger is not afraid. Angry people feed upon the fear of others.

Chapter 9. Influence People With Mind Control

A mind controller approaches the victim with the sole intent of cloning themselves, making the other person think like them. This is a complicated thing to do, so, to achieve it, one has to possess an inflated ego, lack doubts about themselves, and have a high sense of entitlement. All of us are susceptible to manipulation, and what matters is how much effect the mind control will have on us.

Psychologists studying mind control have found out that the entire process seems to adhere to a typical structure. This conclusion was made after a study was conducted on multiple marketing and networking companies which used mind control to persuade clients to purchase their products. One of the remarkable similarities is that all new members joining the companies underwent pre-planned training to recruit more people and convince potential customers to buy their products. The training sessions are meant to make the employees think like the company wants and use a mind twist to convince people.

Let us now look at the mind control process in detail:

Step 1: Understanding the target

Before anything else, the manipulator will seek to establish a bond or connection with their potential victim. Good intent, or friendship, will be the first step because it makes the victim lower all their social and psychological defenses. Once the controller gains the target's trust, they start reading them to devise the most effective method to invade them. The reading aims to tell whether their victim is susceptible to their manipulation. Just like any project manager, they do not like wasting time on a subject they suspect might outsmart them and lead to failure.

Multiple clues are used to scan the victim. They include vocal style, body language, social status, gender, emotional stability, etc. A person's traits can be used to decode the strength of their defenses. All this time, the manipulator will be asking themselves questions like, "Are you introvert or extrovert?" "Are you weakly?" "Are you emotional?" "Are you self-confident?" Humans give a lot of information about themselves when interacting with each other. This is something that the controller knows all too well. From these signs, they can quickly tell if the person is cooperating. They will look at body posture and immediately analyze the victim. Excess blinking might insinuate that a person is lying. Arms folded across the chest might show a lack of interest or insecurity. Taking enormous strides while walking might portray fear. As you can see, the body releases so much data at any given time that it is essential to be aware of the signs that you are giving out

When the attacker has collected enough data from the target, they now understand their interests, strengths, weaknesses, routines, and so on. Using this information, they can decide on an entry point, which will allow for easy and accurate manipulation. They also determine whether the target is worth the effort. If they see one as a favorable target, they move to the other step in the mind control process- unfreezing factual beliefs and values.

Step 2: Unfreezing Solid Beliefs and Values

All of us have some beliefs and values engraved deep within. Most of them are the principles that were instilled in us since childhood, and others have been acquired from experiences are we grow older. We rarely let go of them, but revise them as we proceed. Most of them make up our identities, so we do not like them being interfered with. If these principles are threatened, contradicted, or questioned at any point in time, our natural reaction is to defend them through all means possible. However, if a good-enough reason is given to us, so we voluntarily question them ourselves; we undergo a process known as "unfreezing."

Tons of reasons can lead us to unfreeze: a breakup, the death of a loved one, religious interference, getting evicted from our houses, to mention but a few. These situations force us to seek answers to complex cases, which goes as deep as questioning our sole beliefs and values. Take this, for example:

Way back when I am a teenager, we had some family friends who were solid Christians. It happens that my best friend, who was my exact age, came from this family. His name was Sam. Sam used to tell me about the Bible and its teachings, trying to convince me to accept salvation and live according to its instructions. I remember asking him why he was so insistent on this issue. He would respond that all problems were solvable with saving and that life was much more comfortable and happier. Fast-forward about fifteen years, Sam's mother was diagnosed with breast cancer. They tried all forms of treatment available at the time, but the cancer would grow back. One day, while talking to him about the issue, he looked at me with a pale face and said, "I think what they say about Christianity is not real!" Unsure about what he had just said, I asked him why he thought so. He responded that they had met tens of spiritual leaders for prayers, but his mother's cancer was only getting worse. What's worse, she would not live for more than a year.

Sad as Sam's story is, it makes us realize that some situations in life might force us to question the vital principles that we grow up with. In this case, my best friend had come to doubt the very same religion that he once felt had automatic solutions to all of life's problems. In the very same manner, a manipulator will dig deep into their victim's life to understand their vulnerabilities and exploit them fully. These people will say anything they think their targets would love to hear. Once the victim swallows the manipulator's comfort, there is a shift in power dynamics, and the target is now ready for the manipulation.

Step 3: Reprogramming the Mind

The mind control process seeks to separate the target from their initial beliefs and begin reprogramming their mind. The reprogramming is meant to install the manipulator's beliefs and values into the victim's mind. Apart from distancing the initial principles, the controller also tries their best to make them look wrong or harmful, or the cause of past mishaps in the victim's life. If the victim absorbs this reprogramming, their defense is lowered to zero, and they now become a robot that is ready to accept any operating system that is offered.

During the reprogramming phase, the attacker will ensure the victim has minimal contact with the outside world. They make everyone else appear insignificant to the victim because this raises their opportunity to deposit their malicious principles. This behavior is typical in cults, mostly crafted to sway their followers from mainstream human life. Some cults go as far as controlling their followers' food intake as a way of weakening them. The psychology behind this idea is that a weak person will always turn to the person they feel has the power to protect them or alleviate their suffering. The same happens in relationships, where one partner plays the controlling role. The victimized one has no choice but to adhere to the other. You might wonder why some people put up with violent partners. Still, so far, you must already understand that the problem is more profound than it appears. If you control a person's mind, you can control their lives.

Once the victim has been reprogrammed, the manipulator moves into the final phase of the mind control process known as "freezing."

Step 4: Freezing the New Beliefs and Values

Once the victim has been fed with contrasting principles by the offender, the offender applies tactics to cement the new beliefs into their brains. This is what psychologists call "freezing." The freezing bit is necessary because the controller is aware of the person's original ideas that might clash with their initial ones. As such, they need to force the victim to choose their malicious principles over their old ones. To do this, they might apply any of the following methods.

One of the methods is using the reward/punishment approach. When the victim acts according to the manipulator's demands, they are rewarded. Hopefully, you see the similarity between the freezing process and dog training. The dog is given treats when it follows the trainer's instructions. The trainer aims at solidifying the new skill in the dog by rewarding it. In the future, if the dog is instructed to do the same thing, it will not hesitate since it has been made to think that obeying the command is useful and attracts a reward. The same applies to mind control; when the victim follows, they are made to feel that what they did was right and deserves a reward.

Punishments are the second most-applied approach in the freezing process. If the victim deviates from the controller's commands, they are punished. If we go back to a cult scenario, they usually have defined punishments for violations of terms. During the Holocaust, for instance, any Germans who failed to hail Hitler were punished through imprisonment or death. In the same way, any German who was suspected of protecting the Jews was shot. Hitler understood that by punishing anyone who went against his rules, he would force every German to help him attain his ethnic cleansing objective. The psychological trick used in these situations is that the victim is made to see punishment as justice being served for breaking the rules.

Mind controllers' final method to solidify their manipulation is to transform their victims into their agents. Better put, once the controller feels that the victim's pseudo personality has materialized, they use them to distribute their worldviews. We said that the mind controller's list is to create a replica of themselves in the other person. Therefore, once the controlling process is complete, the victim starts living like the attacker without realizing it. Depending on the manipulation's nature, the victim might also be used to recruit more victims into the oppressor's way of thinking and living. This is especially true in the context of marketing and networking. From this explanation, we can readily tell why a wife is likely to be violent towards the kids if the husband is violent. The kids are also expected to be violent towards each other or their friends. The process of mind control is slow, but once it solidifies, it can result in devastating effects.

Chapter 10. Dark Persuasion

Whenever folks try to provide meaning to the notion of demeanor, their responses always come in various forms. Even though some could put their thoughts on the ads and advertisements which are everywhere in contemporary society, advocating you to patronize a specific product or service over the other others' heads fall back into the politicians who attempt to modify the minds of Republicans simply to get yet another vote in the polls. Both instances are right since they are messages targeted at altering the understanding of this topic. The purpose of diversion between ordinary persuasion and dim persuasion is the dark persuasion doesn't necessarily have a moral rationale.

Even though a standard persuader might attempt to convince someone for this individual's own great, a dim persuader does so together with motives that are not always great for another individual. They try to obtain a total grasp of the individual they would like to convince and take pains to do this since they understand the greatest motivation.

While persuasion consistently has ethical consequences, a dim persuader doesn't concern themselves with those consequences. In reality, they are mindful of these, but decide to put their eyes on their goal (s) rather than persuasion as a mental phenomenon in an individual's regular life. It's either that you're the person attempting to convince someone else or you're being persuaded. What makes the distinction between dark and ordinary is that the motivation for this. In mass media, politics, legal and advertising conclusions, persuasion comes to play all of the time. The results of instructing it in such areas are set utilizing persuasion to determine the topic of influence.

There are a few clear and crucial differences between behavioral and other brain control varieties, like brainwashing and hypnosis. Even though these two demands that the topic should be isolated from modifying their thoughts and individuality, persuasion doesn't require isolation. To be able to reach the target, manipulation is utilized on a single individual. Although persuasion may also be performed on a single topic to make them change their thoughts, there's also a chance of using it on a vast scale to alter the heads of an entire group or a whole society.

Because of this, persuasion is a much better mind control procedure and maybe more harmful since it can alter the minds of lots of people at precisely the same time rather than the head of only one individual at one time. Many people produce the error of believing that they have immunity to the consequences of persuasion because they think that they will always have the ability to observe every sales pitch that comes in their way.

They think they'll always have the ability to use logic to grasp what's happening and find a logical decision for this. As a result of how people aren't ever likely to fall for whatever they hear, this might be accurate if they utilize logic. It's likewise feasible to steer clear of persuasion since the debate doesn't augur nicely with the individual's beliefs, whatever the strength of this debate. Some individuals understand how to use clear messages to inspire people to market the industry's newest gadgets or goods. This information action is quite delicate, so the topic won't always recognize it; therefore, it's going to be rather difficult for them to continually have the ability to decide the information they will get.

Every time is said, it's extremely probable that you think about it in a terrible light. That is because it is inclined to automatically consider a conman or salesman who's always attempting to make them modify their view, and that will finally push them till this shift is reached. While black persuasion is notable in earnings and conning clinics, also, there are ways that persuasion may be used permanently, such as in diplomatic relationships between global bodies or at public service attempts. The difference only lies in the method by which in which the practice of persuasion is attracted to perform.

Dark Persuasion Methods

When an individual is prepared to modify the head of the topic by devoting them to do anything against their first frame of mind, the persuader will get some nicely laid out methods to help them reach their targets. Every day that passes, the goal will face various kinds of persuasion. Food manufacturers aim to receive their goal to test the recipes that are new or have them adhere to the earlier ones, even while studios may flaunt their most recent blockbuster films about the faces of the aims. In any situation may be whatever merchandise they're promoting, their principal intent is to generate more revenue, and that's the reason they're attempting to convince you. They couldn't care less about how this may affect you, and that is why they need to be quite careful and proficient in the art of subtle persuasion to make sure they don't deceive you off or make you plump.

As there are also lots of different brands attempting to convince you, they need to locate an exceptional approach to impress their perspectives on you. As a result of the effect of info on a vast selection of individuals, the methods used in it's been a topic of research for several decades, dating back to early times. That is because the influence is a really helpful instrument in controlling a large assortment of individuals. Beginning in the early 20th century, the proper analysis of those techniques started to grow. Bear in mind that the objective of attempting to convince people would be to push a compelling debate in an audience and have the positive.

They'll then internalize this information and embrace it as their fresh mindset or even means of life. Because of this, there's a great need to find very prosperous persuasion methods. Three dark persuasion methods are of fantastic value through recent years. We will go over those three:

Create a Need

This is only one of the most profitable methods of obtaining an individual to change their perspective or lifestyle. The individual hoping to convince a goal will create demand or concentrate on a demand that the topic already has. If that is achieved suitably, it's the capacity of enticing a fantastic deal to your goal. This signifies that to become prosperous, the persuader should interest in the demands that are far more significant to the goal.

This could be their requirement to fulfill their fantasies of fostering their self-esteem. It might also function as a desire for love, food, or shelter. This method will work out nicely since there's not anyway the topic isn't likely to require one or more of these items or need of anything at all for that matter. As there's not always, the goal is not likely to get dreams and ambitions. The persuader will probably simply find strategies to produce the sufferer understand how they can easily help the sufferer attain those dreams. The persuader can also tell their goal the goal will probably recognize their visions if they make certain adjustments to their faith or outlook.

As stated by the persuader, doing this will provide the target with a greater prospect of attaining success. For example, a young guy who wishes to get romantic with a woman may inform her that he'll help her boost her grades and eventually make her parents happy by obtaining a. Still, only when she's friends with his or her although this woman may believe she has finally discovered the salvation she desires, the simple truth is that the young guy is not very curious about how she plays in college. Her teenagers are just a lure for obtaining access to sexual activity.

Appealing to Social Needs

Another technique the persuader may utilize is identifying the goal of social demands. Even though this might not yield as many outcomes and the goal's main requirements will, it's still a powerful instrument in the hands of the persuader. Some are naturally attracted to audiences and want to be desired. They always wish for certain things, not because they want them, but because it includes certain prestige, making them feel like they belong to a bigger course. The idea of appealing to your target's societal needs is what's accessible through several TV advertisements where audiences are invited to purchase a product so they won't be "left behind." When they could recognize and allure to the societal needs of their goal, the outcome is that they can achieve a new field of the goal's interest.

Making Use of Loaded Words and Images

When an individual is hoping to convince someone else, they need to be cautious with their selection of words because words could make all of the difference. When there are many means to say something, one way of stating it might be more potent than another. When it's related to persuasion, among the essential things is understanding how to say the ideal thing at the ideal moment. Words are the most effective tools in communicating and understanding the perfect call-to-action phrases.

Dark persuasion is just one of the most effective dim psychology theories, but regrettably, it's always overlooked and suppressed. This might be because, unlike many different head control procedures, persuasion renders the goal using a selection. At another mind control procedure, the aim is forced to enter.

Occasionally, this is achieved by placing them into isolation to ensure, in conclusion, they don't have any say in the procedure results. Regarding persuasion, the chips have been laid bare (though with the ulterior purpose in dim persuasion), so the goal is made to make the choice they think will fit them best.

Chapter 11. Dark Persuasion To Lookout For

After looking at the different types of persuasion and what they all mean, you may see why dark persuasion is such a bad thing and can be harmful to the victim. Recognizing the different techniques that the manipulator may use can make it easier to understand when used on you.

So, how exactly is a dark persuader able to use this idea to carry out their wishes? There are a few different types of tactics that a dark manipulator is going to use. Still, some of the most common options include:

The Long Con

The first method that we are going to look at is the Long Con. This method is kind of slow and drawn out, but it can be effective because it takes so long, and it is hard to recognize or pinpoint when something went wrong. One of the main reasons that some people can resist persuasion is that they feel that they are being pressured by the other person, making them back off. If they feel that there is a lack of rapport or trust with the person trying to persuade them, they will steer clear. The Long Con is effective because they can overcome these main problems and give the persuader precisely what they want.

The Long Con will involve the dark persuader to take their time, working to earn their victim's trust. They will take some time to befriend the victim and make sure that their victims trust and like them. The persuader will achieve this with artificial rapport building, which sometimes seems excessive, and other techniques will help increase the comfort levels between the persuader and their victim.

As soon as the persuader sees that the victim is adequately readied psychologically, the persuader will begin their attempts. They may start with some insincere positive persuasion. The persuader will lead their victim to choose or do some activities that will benefit the persuader. This is going to serve the persuader in two ways. First, the victim starts to become used to persuasion by that persuader. The second is that the victim will start making that mental association between a positive outcome and the persuasion.

The Long Con will take a long period to complete because the persuader doesn't want to make it too obvious what they are doing. An example of this is a victim who is a recently widowed lady who is vulnerable because of her age and from their grief. After her loss, a man starts to befriend her. This man may be someone she knows from church or even a relative. He starts to spend more time with her, showing immense kindness and patience, and it doesn't take too long for her guard to drop when he comes around.

Then this man starts to carry out some smaller acts of positive persuasion that we talked about before. He may advise her of a better bank account to use or a better way to reduce any monthly bills. The victim will appreciate these efforts and the fact that the man is trying to help her, and she takes the advice.

Over some time, the man then tries to use some dark persuasion. He may try to persuade her to let him invest some of her money. She obliges because of the positive persuasion that was used in the past. Of course, the man is going to work to take everything he can get from her. If the manipulator is skilled enough, she may feel that he actually tried to help her, but the money is lost because he just ran into some bad luck with the investment. This is how far dark persuasion can go.

Graduality

Often when we hear about acts of dark persuasion, it seems impossible and unbelievable. They fail to realize that this dark persuasion isn't ever going to be a big or a sudden request that comes out of nowhere. Dark persuasion is more like a staircase. The dark persuader will never ask the victim to do something big and dramatic the first time they meet. Instead, they will have the victim take one step at a time.

When the manipulator has the target only go one step at a time, the whole process seems like less of a big deal. Before the victim knows it, they have already gone a long way down, and the persuader isn't likely to let them leave or come back up again.

Let's take an example of how this process is going to look in real life. Let's say that there is a criminal who wanted to make it so that someone else committed the crimes for them. Gang bosses, cult leaders, and even Charles Manson did this same thing.

This criminal wouldn't dream of beginning the process by asking their victim to murder for them. This would send out a red flag, and no one in their right minds would willingly go out and kill for someone they barely know. Instead, the criminal would start by having the victim do something small, like a petty crime, or simply hiding a weapon for them. Something that isn't that big of a deal for the victim, at least in comparison.

Over time, the acts that the manipulator can persuade their victim to do will become more severe. And since they did the smaller crimes, the persuader now has the unseen leverage of holding some of those smaller misdeeds over the victim, kind of like for blackmail. Before the victim knows it, they are going to feel like they are in too deep. They will then be persuaded to carry out some of the most shocking crimes. And often, by this point, they will do it because they feel like they have no other choice.

Dark persuaders will be experts at using this graduality to help increase the severity of their persuasion over time. They know that no victim would be willing to jump the canyon or do the big crime or misdeed right away. So, the persuader works to build a bridge to get there. By the time the victim sees how far they are, it is too late to turn back.

Masking the True Intentions

There are different methods that a persuader can use dark psychology to get the things that they want. Disguising their true desires is very important for them to be successful. The best persuaders can use this approach in various ways. Still, the method they choose is often going to depend on the victim and the situation.

One principle used by a persuader is that many people will have a difficult time refusing two requests when they happen in a row. Let's say that the persuader wants to get $200 from the victim, but they do not intend to repay the money. The persuader may begin by saying that they need a loan for the amount of $1000. They may go into some details about the consequences to themselves if the persuader doesn't come up with that kind of money sometime soon.

The victim may feel guilt or compassion for the persuader, and they want to help. But $1000 is a lot of money, more than the victim can lend. From here, the persuader is going to lessen their request from $1000 down to $200, the amount that they wanted from the beginning. Of course, there is some emotional reason for needing the money. The victim feels like it is impossible to refuse this second request. They want to help out the persuader, and they feel bad for not giving in to the initial request when they were asked. In the end, the persuader gets the $200 they originally wanted, and the victim is not going to know what has taken place.

Another type of technique that the persuader can use is known as reverse psychology. This can also help to mask true intentions during the persuasion. Some people have a personality that is known as a boomerang. This means that they will refuse to go in the direction they are thrown away and instead will veer off into different directions.

If the persuader knows someone more of a boomerang type, they can identify a key weakness. For example, let's say that a persuader has a friend attempting to win over some girl they like. The persuader knows that the friend will use and then hurt that girl. The girl is currently torn between a malicious friend and an innocent third party. The persuader may try to steer the girl in the direction of the guy who is a good choice, knowing that she will go against this and end up going with the harmful friend.

Leading Questions

Another method of dark persuasion that can be used is known as leading questions. If you have ever had an encounter with a skilled salesman, verbal persuasion can be really impactful when deployed in careful and calibrated ways. One of the most powerful techniques that can be used verbally is leading questions.

These leading questions will be any questions intended to trigger a specific response out of the victim. The persuader may ask the target something like, "how bad do you think those people are?" This question will imply that the people the persuader is asking about are bad to some extent. They could have chosen to ask a non-leading question, such as "how do you feel about those people?"

Dark persuaders are masters at using leading questions in a way that is hard to catch. If the victim ever begins to feel that they are being led, they will resist, and it is hard to lead them or persuade them. If a persuader ever senses that their victim starts to catch what is happening, they will quit using that one and switch over to another. They may come back to that tactic, but only when the victim has quieted down a bit and is more influenceable again.

The Law of State Transference

The state is a concept that will take a look at the general mood someone is in. If someone is aligned with their deeds, words, and thoughts, this is an example of a healthy and harmonious state. The law of state transference will involve the concept of someone who holds the balance of power in a situation and can then transfer their emotional state onto the other person they interact with. This can be a potent tool for the dark persuader to use against their victim.

Initially, the influencer will force their state to match the state that their target naturally has. If the target is sad and talks slowly, the influencer will make their state follow this format. The point of this is to create a deep rapport with the target.

After we get to this state match, the influencer will alter their state subtly and see if they have some compliance for the victim. Perhaps they will choose to speed up their voice to see if the victim will speed up as well. Once the victim starts to show these signs of compliance, the influencer is at the hook point.

Chapter 12. Subliminal Persuasion

S ubliminal persuasion means an advertising message displayed below the threshold of awareness or consumer awareness to persuade or help people change their minds without making them aware of what is going on. This is about affecting individuals with more than words. Some subliminal persuasion methods impact our stimuli with smell, eyesight, sound, touch, and taste.

There are 3 subliminal methods of persuasion that affect everyone. They are:

Building a Relationship

Building a relationship makes the other person feel comfortable. This will open up the individual even more. This can be accomplished through a healthy observation that matches their mood or state. This helps create confidence.

Power of Discussion

The power of discussion and convincing a person is connected to an advertiser's conversion. The correct words and inflections help you to be openly straightforward.

Suggestive Power

Associating useful and desirable stuff in a discussion or interaction enables an individual to become more open to fresh thoughts.

Suggestion and Emotional Intelligence

This stage may be described as having one central and dominant idea focused on the participant's conscious mind, which was to stimulate or decrease the various regions' physiological performance within the participant's body. Using different nonverbal and verbal suggestions was increasingly emphasized to convince the participant easily.

Achieve Optimal Persuasion With Subliminal Psychology

When you can expertly utilize a person's subconscious depths, your control over them is easy and vast. Subliminal psychology is one of the most effective ways to do this. This is an advanced technique, so do not expect to become effective overnight, but know that with time and dedication, you will be able to start putting subliminal messages into the minds of those around you. Once you can do this, you will control what they think and the actions they take. Essentially, you become almost like a puppet master for those around you.

Subliminal Message Techniques

This type of message or affirmation presented either visually or auditory sent in a way below what is considered normal for human visual or auditory perception. For example, a record might be playing on repeat, but you cannot hear it with your conscious mind. However, deep in your subconscious, you hear it and fully register everything that it is saying. In most cases, the messages used are meant to control you in some way or suggest that you do something.

For example, subliminal messages are commonly used in today's world to promote smoking cessation or weight loss. In general, you listen to recorded tapes with a specific message when you are sleeping. Your unconscious mind gets the message, but you never really hear it as your conscious self. Either way, research shows that it can be an effective tool to change your smoking or eating behaviors. You can use a similar technique to help change how people think to make them more vulnerable to the types of persuasion you prefer to use.

This is an effective way to control both your mind and others' minds, but it can be obvious when you do not use the techniques properly. As you read into the primary techniques, pay close attention to how you might introduce a person to them. This is important. Ultimately, your relationship with the person you are seeking to control will determine which of these techniques works the best.

Subliminal Messages During Sleep

This is one of the most common ways to use these types of messages. Most people will use them for themselves in this manner, but you can also use them with people you live with. For example, once you know your spouse is asleep, play a subliminal recording for about one hour. This is all it takes to get your message across.

Now, you must know for sure that they are sleeping, or else you could do more harm than good to your persuasion efforts. When you create your recording, use a calm and steady voice. State precisely what you want the person to do. Use no filler words. Use a maximum of 10 words and simply repeat it for an hour. Then, once the person is sleeping, play the recording at a very low volume close to their head so that their unconscious mind hears it.

Subliminal Flashes

These do not take as long as they are not as risky as the above method. These are a type of visual subliminal message. You can create the flashes to say what you want. What is nice about this technique is that the messages flash so quickly that the conscious mind often does not see what it says. Only the subconscious can understand and record it. So, you can get some control over a person's mind without them knowing what you are attempting to control.

Unless the person you want to do this with knows about subliminal psychology, you can just tell them you want to show them something you created. It is best to do this on a computer so that the screen is large enough to read and keep their full attention during the flashes.

Mixed Subliminal Messages

You can insert subliminal messages into the music or audiobooks that someone listens to regularly. Some programs can do this, so you do not have to be a tech expert to take advantage of this method. Just like with the subliminal messages during sleep, you will use a calm and steady voice. You want the messages to mix into the audiobook or music without being detected. Remember, the subconscious mind will pick up on it even when they cannot hear it when they are awake.

Just make sure to use these messages in something they listen to daily, or almost daily. They must hear it regularly to gain the most control.

Subliminal Notes

This is the easiest method, but it is also the simplest to figure out if you are not careful. You can put messages inside messages throughout your home. For example, when you create the grocery list, add something else you want but do not usually shop for. This puts the thought in the person's head when they are reading the list. This is ideal for smaller things that you want to persuade someone to think or do. So, keep it simple and use this method periodically. Unlike the above methods, it is not a good idea to use it every day.

Chapter 13. Psychological Manipulation

T oday, the greatest battles are not fought on battlefields but in our minds and hearts!

And one of the biggest and strongest reasons for an inner battle is psychological manipulation. The biggest problem with psychological manipulation is not only the fact that we are often not prepared to deal with it but also the way we respond to it. And then, our greatest enemy, beyond the manipulator/oppressor, will become ourselves!

One of the main characteristics of psychological manipulation is that the manipulator (who can be a father, a mother, a brother or sister, a romantic partner, or a friend) exercises great control and power over us. And in that instant, our life becomes a real hell, and we live in tremendous anguish.

However, it is crucial to know that we are not, and should not be, impotent in this situation. There are various ways of combating these techniques of psychological manipulation.

The first step is to achieve consciousness, that is, to become aware of these techniques. Take a closer look and learn more objectively how your handlers "work" so you can protect yourself in the future. There are several Manipulation Techniques. See some of them below:

Psychological Manipulation Technique 1: Emotional Blackmail

Emotional blackmail is one of the oldest and most used manipulation techniques employed by human beings. But how does this work exactly?

Many people succumb to this trick because they feel they have no choice. At this point, phrases such as "If you cared about me, you would do this for me" are very common and make the manipulated person feel "forced" to make decisions they do not want. The target will make them anyway just to please the person who manipulates.

To avoid this manipulation technique, you will have to develop a strong sense of yourself, which involves knowing who you are, what your responsibilities are towards others, and who your true friends are. Usually, manipulative and blackmailing people tend to stay away from people with strong and solid personalities. Always remember: you always have a choice, and it is you who decides what you do with your life and how you want to react to the world.

Psychological Manipulation Technique 2: Focus on Negative Aspects

Some people like to put a "brake" on another's ideas and brilliant projects by emphasizing everything that could go wrong with them. These people often push him to doubt his projects and all the good things they would bring if they were put into practice. And at these times, the manipulators offer an endless list of questions that will only serve to create and raise doubts in their target's mind and heart.

For example, if you tell someone, you are thinking of traveling somewhere for a month to relax or go on vacation. If that person does not feel comfortable with the idea for some reason, they will probably react to your news by talking about the big travel hazards and the endless number of negative things that can be expected at the airport, etc.

At such times, if there is no apparent reason for such a reaction from the other person. If you are comfortable with your decision, bearing in mind that it will not harm you or others, choose not to listen to them and follow through with what you have decided.

Do not be overly swayed by this negative thinking pattern. If we think about something a lot, we attract it. If you put it in your head that something bad will happen and focus on it excessively, it is very likely to happen because the thought has life and is a great magnet.

Psychological Manipulation Technique 3: Teenage Rebellion

Unfortunately, sometimes the manipulative person adopts a childlike attitude to respond to his decision or something you have said to him.

For example, you want to leave your home and live independently. At first, it may even seem like everyone is happy and comfortable with your decision. But with time, as soon as you start looking for the perfect apartment, things start happening one after another. Some personal crisis occurs in the family, your mother or father suddenly (re)starts smoking, etc. These are adult people, but they adopt the behavior of a teenager and rebel against the idea.

The easiest way to deal with this is to make them see that their efforts to make you give up are worthless and that you will go ahead with your decision.

At first, it can be challenging and hard for you, especially if you have been exposed to this type of psychological manipulation for a long time. But as time goes by, it will become much easier, and you will see that even the people who manipulate you will come to respect you much more.

Psychological manipulation can be done throughout life, but always remember that you have the power to break this vicious cycle, and above all, remember that only one person can change your life: You!

Love and life together can be sources of well-being, pleasure, and support or a dead-end in which you feel suffocated and as if you are in the dark. The worst is that in many cases, these can be combined in a single day. Both feelings and problems begin when the relationship shifts rapidly. You find yourself immersed in a constant storm of feelings. This mainly happens to those who do not know how to escape such situations.

Many people are immersed in insane and toxic relationships in which they suffer psychological abuse of various kinds. They receive continuous damage to their integrity and honor and levels of disrespect that seem crazy when seen or heard from outside. Still, to the person who is now accustomed to suffering, they do not even produce a minimal reaction in their daily lives.

Love is not an excuse to hide the emotional pain that another person can cause us. It is our responsibility to ourselves to learn how to defend our rights and enforce them. Beyond your insecurity, the parental patterns that you picked up in your childhood, and all the mechanisms of self-deception that you can activate so as not to see reality, at the bottom of your being, you know how to differentiate what is right and what hurts you. That said, sometimes we need someone to tell us in a neutral and unbiased way that we have the right not to put up with what we know we do not deserve. Present a list of the main techniques of manipulation in unhealthy couples.

Manipulation to maintain social control: This technique usually begins in a very subtle way. The couple criticizes friends, family, work colleagues, and anyone in your social circle until they can completely annul the other's social network in such a way that the only source of effort and social support is the couple. This is manifested through jealousy: "If you love me, you would prefer me over your friends," etc. Emotional blackmail: This mechanism is famous for being used between pairs of individuals. It is also widely used by almost everyone, and you likely know it very well. It is about using phrases to handle guilt and repentance as a tactic to get something or as an impediment so that the other does not do something or does not abandon the manipulator. The manipulative person usually uses phrases like: "If you do that, it means you don't love me," "I do not want you to suffer, I would never do that to you," "I want the best for you, even if you let me destroy my life," "If you let me die," etc.

Chapter 14. Psychological Manipulation Technique

What Are Manipulators Looking For

Deceptive people in general: sociopaths, narcissists, liars, and so-called emotional vampires, and it is more a practical question to consider them than a theoretical one. For this purpose, if you've been victims of them at times, it's easier for you to identify and precede them now.

However, it can be said that deceptive people's aims are very straightforward, instrumental and that they follow a specific pattern. Most of them include:

- **Cancel your willpower**: they're trying to sow suspicions and want to bind you to their safety.

- Destroying your self-esteem: bringing a spoken word into the wheel of all you do or have done. We are not helpful and just want to point out the shortcomings.

- Passive-aggressive revenge: By avoiding you, they threaten you. They neglect you when you need them; it's enough to ask something, to get to stand up and not even speak to you.

- Prevent reality: they enjoy confounding people and creating misunderstandings and discussions. We step back after provoking a debate, loving the rants of others.

-

What Are the Psychological Manipulation Techniques?

Gaslighting

Gaslighting is one of the most subtle methods of deception. "It's never happened," "Imagine you" or " You're kidding?" These are some of the words that they use to manipulate and confuse our perception of reality, making us believe things have changed.

This instills an intense sense of anxiety and uncertainty in the victims, to the point of causing them not to trust in themselves, their memory, their understanding, or their judgment.

Projection

The manipulator transfers the negative characteristics to another person or shifts blame for his actions. This is being used heavily by narcissists and psychopaths, saying that the wickedness surrounding them is not their fault but anyone else's.

Meaningless Conversations

The conversation lasts ten minutes. Now is the time for you to leave the conversation. Manipulators say ridiculous things, offer illogical excuses, refer to past events, and throw smoke in the eyes...

We generate discord and misunderstanding. We are doing monologues, and they are trying to confuse you with their gab. Some advice? Get straight to the point and then better if you can leave after 5 minutes. Your feelings would be thankful.

Generalizations and Denigrations

They make generic, vague, and abstract statements. They may seem intellectual. In reality, they are just elusive. Their conclusions are too general; their goal is to demean your e debilitate your opinions.

For example, "you always want to be right," "anything annoys you," "never once you agree." Keep calm. You can opt for irony, with a simple "thank you," or you can ignore them with a curt, "I think you're a little upset. We'll talk later."

Absurdity

Remember that they try to undermine your morals and cause you to question what you believe. They can put words you have never said in your mouth; they will make you think you have the superpower to "read your mind." But that's not the case, and they are just tricks and deceptions. You can help yourself with simulated defeat. Tell them they are right for them to believe it, but stick to your position. You can also respond to their blackmail with an "okay" or with harsh sentences.

The important thing is that you take your self-esteem out of their hands. Remember that they want to demoralize you so that they can control you. After making you weak, the task will be much easier.

Good Mask

"Yes, but..." If you manage to buy a house, they will tell you that it is a pity that you do not yet have a place by the sea; if you are dressed more elegant than ever, they will tell you that another pair of earrings would have been better for you. If you have written an impeccable report, they will tell you that the staple is not well fixed.

But don't let yourselves be influenced: you know what you are worth! Your successes and virtues are worth more than their manipulation techniques. Don't give them any credibility and hang out with people who spend more time pointing out the positives and encouraging you; those who compliment you when you deserve them and who make constructive, non-destructive criticisms.

Positive Reinforcement

Through positive reinforcement learning, behavioral performance is linked to achieving a good outcome. This does not have to be an entity, not even tangible; in many cases, food, liquids, a smile, a verbal message, or the presence of a friendly emotion are likely to be seen as favorable reinforcement.

A father who congratulates his young daughter if she uses the toilet correctly promotes positive reinforcement learning; the same thing happens when a business offers cash incentives to its most successful workers. When we get a bag of potato chips after placing a coin into a retailer.

The definition of "positive reinforcement" refers to the reward that accompanies the action. In contrast, positive reinforcement is the process that creates the connection the learner produces. Nevertheless, the words "reinforcement" and "reinforcement" are frequently used interchangeably, possibly because such a distinction does not exist in English.

From a technical point of view, we can conclude a favorable variance between a particular response and an appetizing stimulus in positive reinforcement. The knowledge of this risk motivates the subject to act to get the reward (or strengthening).

Negative Reinforcement

In comparison to what occurs in the positive, the instrumental response in the negative reinforcement includes the absence of an aversive stimulus, i.e., an event or condition that motivates the subject to avoid or attempt not to come into contact with it.

In behavioral terms, the reinforcement of this technique is the absence or non-appearance of the aversive stimulus. As we stated earlier, the word "negative" refers to the fact that the reward does not consist of obtaining inspiration but in the absence thereof.

This type of learning is divided into two processes: training to escape and train to prevent it. The conduct precludes the presence of the aversive stimulus in the negative reinforcement of avoidance. For example, when an agoraphobic individual avoids using public transport to escape the fear this presupposes, it is reinforced negatively.

On the contrary, the escape is the disappearance of an aversive stimulus present before the subject executes the behavior. Some examples of negative escape reinforcement include an alarm clock that stops by pressing a button, a mother buying a request for her child to stop weeping, or taking a pain reliever to relieve pain.

Brainwashing

The concept of brainwashing is very close to that of 'mind control.' It is an idea without a strictly scientific basis that suggests that the will, thoughts, and other mental facts of individuals can be modified through techniques of persuasion that would introduce unwanted ideas into the psyche of the 'victim.' If we define the concept in this way, we see that it has a marked similarity. However, the term "suggest" is less ambitious.

Although the idea of brainwashing is not entirely wrong, this popular concept has some scientific connotations which have led many experts to reject it in favor of more modest ones. The instrumental use of the term in legal proceedings has contributed to this, particularly in child custody disputes.

Mind control is also known as brainwashing, coercive persuasion, mind control, and mental manipulation. All these terms mean a process that a group or individual systematically uses to force someone to do what they want through thinking of that person. In the majority of cases, these systematic processes are realized without the conscious knowledge of the person.

There are times when we can use mind control over ourselves for a variety of reasons. Self-hypnosis is in this category. We use this kind of mind control, which is voluntary on our part, with our conscious consent, to reinforce a positive idea or to change our minds.

However, this is not the same as the "mind control" phase, or it involves brainwashing. These phrases mean that a person's mind is systematically changed without knowing it, either in the agreement or against his will.

They are carried out through unethical, manipulative tactics, and other means, all designed to control someone's mind. In such cases, they are realized so that one person or group can take full control of others' thoughts and actions. So, when the terms "mind control" and "brainwashing" are used, it is said that specific tactics are used to take control of another at the expense of the manipulated person.

This is interesting because the idea of brainwashing falls under the category of social influence. This is because the concept of brainwashing is used to induce a victim's mental manipulation. This means that brainwashing and mind control are used to completely change how someone thinks and perceives things concerning their beliefs in a particular social device. This is achieved by using various means to change a person's attitudes, behaviors, and thoughts. The person is like a puppet who does everything the manipulator wants.

Chapter 15. Covert Emotional Manipulation

C overt emotional manipulation is used by people who want to gain power or control over you by deploying deceptive and underhanded tactics. Such people want to change the way you think and behave without realizing what they are doing. In other words, they use techniques that can alter your perceptions in such a way that you think that you are doing it out of your own free will. Covert emotional manipulation is "covert" because it works without you being consciously aware of that fact. People who are good at deploying such techniques can get you to do their bidding without your knowledge; they can hold you "psychologically captive."

When skilled manipulators set their sights on you, they can get you to grant them power over your emotional well-being and even your self-worth. They will put you under their spell without you even realizing it. They will win your trust, and you will start attaching value to what they think of you. Once you have let them into your life, they will then begin to chipping away at your very identity in a systematic way. As time goes by, you will lose your self-esteem and turn into whatever they want you to be.

Covert emotional manipulation is more common than you might think. Since it's subtle, people are rarely aware that it's happening to them, and in some cases, they may never even notice. Only keen outside observers may be able to tell when this form of manipulation is going on.

You might know someone who used to be fun and festive. She got into a relationship with someone else, and a few years down the line, she seems to have a completely different personality. If it's an old friend, you might not even recognize the person she has become. That is how powerful covert emotional manipulation can be. It can completely overhaul someone's personality without them even realizing it. The manipulator will chip away at you little by little. You will accept minute changes that fly under the radar until the old a different version of you replaces you, build to be subservient to the manipulator.

Covert emotional manipulation works like a slow-moving coup. It requires you to make small progressive concessions to the person that is trying to manipulate you. In other words, you let go of tiny aspects of your identity to accommodate the manipulative person, so it never registers in your mind that there is something bigger at play.

When the manipulative person pushes you to change in small ways, you will comply because you don't want to "sweat the small stuff." However, there is a domino effect that occurs as you start conceding to the manipulative person. You will be more comfortable making subsequent concessions, and your personality will be erased and replaced in a cumulative progression.

Covert emotional manipulation occurs to some extent in all social dynamics. Let's look at how it plays out in romantic relationships, in friendships, and at work.

Emotional Manipulation in Relationships

There is a lot of emotional manipulation in romantic relationships, and it's not always malicious. For example, women try to modify men's behavior to make them more "housebroken";

that is just normal. However, certain instances of manipulation where the person's intention is malicious, and he/she is motivated by a need to control or dominate over the other person.

Positive reinforcement is perhaps the most used covert manipulation technique in romantic relationships. Your partner can get you to do what he wants by praising you, flattering you, giving you attention, offering your gifts, and acting affectionately.

Even the seemingly nice things in relationships can turn out to be covert manipulation tools and props. For instance, your girlfriend could use intense sex as a weapon to reinforce a certain kind of behavior in you. Similarly, men can use charm, appreciation, or gifts to reinforce certain behaviors in the women they are dating.

Some sophisticated manipulators use what psychologists call "intermittent positive reinforcement" to gain control over their partners. The way it works is that the perpetrator will shower the victim with intense positive reinforcement for a certain period, then switch to just giving her normal levels of attention and appreciations. After a random interval of time, he will again go back to the intense positive reinforcement. When the victim gets used to the special treatment, it's taken away. When she gets used to standard therapy, the special treatment is brought back, and it all seems arbitrary. Now, the victim will get to a place where she becomes "addicted" to the special treatment. Still, she has no idea how to get it. Hence, she starts doing whatever the perpetrator wants, hoping that one of the things she does will bring back the intense positive reinforcement. In other words, she effectively becomes subservient to the perpetrator.

Negative reinforcement techniques are also used in relationships to manipulate others covertly. For example, partners can withhold sex to compelling the other person to modify their behavior in a specific way. People also use techniques such as the silent treatment and withholding of love and affection.

Some malicious people can create a false sense of intimacy by pretending to open up to you. They could share personal stories and talk about their hopes and fears. When they do this, they create the impression that they trust you, but their intention may be to get you to feel a sense of obligation towards them.

Manipulators also use well-calculated insinuations to get you to react in a certain way at the moment to modify your behavior in the long run. Such insinuations can be made through words or even actions. In colloquial terms, we call this "dropping a hint." People in relationships are always trying to figure out what the other person wants out of that relationship, so a manipulative person can drop hints to get you to do what they want without ever having to take responsibility for the actions that you take because they can always argue that you misinterpreted what they meant.

Dropping hints isn't always malicious (for example, if your girlfriend wants you to propose, she may leave bridal magazines out on the table). However, malicious insinuations can be very hurtful, and they can chip away at your self-esteem. Your partner can make insinuations to suggest you are gaining weight. You aren't making enough money or implying that your cooking skills aren't any good. People use hints to get away with "saying without saying," any number of hurtful things that could affect your self-esteem.

Emotional Manipulations in Friendships

Covert emotional manipulation is quite common in friendships and casual relationships. Companies tend to progress slower than romantic relationships, but that just means that it can take a lot more time for you to figure out if your friends are manipulative. Manipulation in friendships can be confusing because even well-meaning friends can come across as malicious. That's because there is a certain social rivalry between even the closest friends, which explains the concept of "frenemies."

Manipulative friends tend to be passive-aggressive. This is where they manipulate you into doing what they want by involving mutual friends rather than directly coming to you. Passive aggression works as a manipulation technique because it denies you a chance of directly addressing whatever issue your friend is raising. So in a manner of speaking, you lose by default.

For example, if a friend wants you to do her a favor, instead of coming out and asking you, she goes to a mutual friend and suggests that she asks you on her behalf. When a mutual friend approaches you, it becomes very difficult for you to turn down the request because of added social pressure. When you say no, your whole social circle now perceives you as selfish.

Passive aggression can also involve the use of silent treatment to get you to comply with a request. Imagine a situation where one of your friends talks to everyone else but you. It's going to be incredibly awkward for you, and everyone will start prying, wondering what the issue is between the two of you, and taking sides on the matter.

Friends can also covertly manipulate you by using subtle insults. They can give you back-handed compliments that have hidden meanings. When you take the time to think about what they meant by the compliment, you will realize that it's an insult in disguise, which will bruise your self-esteem and possibly modify your behavior.

Some friends can manipulate you by going on a "power trip" and controlling your social interactions. For example, there are those friends who insist that every time you hang out, it should be in their apartment or at a social venue of their choosing. Such friends often intend to dominate your friendship, so they are keen to always have the "home ground advantage" over you. They'll try to push you out of your comfort zone just so that you can reveal your weaknesses, and you can then become more emotionally reliant on them.

Manipulative friends tend to excessively capitalize on your friendship, and to a disproportionate degree. They will ask you for lots of favors with no regard for your time or your effort. They are the kinds of friends who will leverage your friendship every time they need something but then make excuses when it's their turn to reciprocate.

Emotional Manipulation at Work

There are many reasons why your colleague may want to manipulate you. It could be you are on the same career path, so he wants to make you look bad. It could be that he is lazy, and he wants to stick you with his responsibilities. It could also be that he is a sadist, and he just wants to see you suffer.

One-way people at work exert their dominance over others is by stressing them out and then, almost immediately, relieving the stress. Say, for example, you make a minor error on a report, and your boss calls you into his office. He makes a big fuss and threatens to fire you, but then towards the end, he switches gears and reassures you that your job is secure as long as you do what he wants. That kind of manipulation works on people because it makes them afraid and gives them a sense of obligation at the same time.

Some colleagues can manipulate you by doing you small favors and then reminding you of those favors every time they want something from you. For instance, if you made an error at work and a colleague covered for you, he may hold it over your head for months or even years to come. He is going to guilt you into feeling indebted to him.

Chapter 16. Covert Emotional Manipulation Tactics

D ark Psychology also spends time looking at Covert Emotional Manipulation. It is more commonly referred to as CEM. CEM is a way to gain real power over someone without them, even realizing it is happening. You will be so enthralled that these sneaky tactics will have you doing things you would not usually agree to.

We have already talked about manipulation, but there are so many different forms of it, which is pretty important. It allows criminals and people with mal intent into your life and breaks you down mentally. The effects of this type of manipulation can last forever if you are not careful. As noted, it is insanely subtle, which means looking for the red flags are very important.

Covert Emotional Manipulation looks different depending on the people involved. Often, the victim will be slowly made to feel like they can't do anything without the other. It is a strange sort of codependency that happens over time. This happens without manipulation on occasion; the difference is when your partner intentionally gets you to behave or think differently.

It may start with offers of help for simple tasks that you usually do on your own. They may follow it up with a critique to make you question your ability to do it. It starts small, but they will continue to poke at it until you start to believe you can't do it on your own truth. You can see it worked into all kinds of things and a ton of relationships.

Depending on who you have allowed doing this to you, it could be mostly harmless. On the other hand, many people with less than genuine intentions could take this to an extreme. This type of manipulation can turn it to flat out brainwashing. In that case, you may lose your free will forever.

People that use CEM against other people pay great attention to detail. This can be endearing as it appears as if they are learning about you. In reality, they are observing your behavior, understanding what makes you tick. This will grant them access to how to manipulate your emotions subtly to get what they want. They are truly hunting for your weaknesses.

The heinous people and criminals that do this in life are calculating. They tend to have bigger plans, and you are simply playing a role. They have no care or regard for how you feel or for the damage they are causing you. All they can see is the outcome that they are striving for. Finding that they are unable ever to sustain relationships is not surprising because of the selfish nature of how they are wired.

As time goes on, CEM turns into something else. What started as little jabs that looked like they were made from love become something much darker. As you start to lose control and bend your will, the aggressor will pounce. They can become domineering. Also, they will begin to tear you down piece by piece to gain complete control.

Playing with someone's emotions is a great way to gain control over them. Some people would rather bombard someone with love to get them to do what they want, rather than being crasser or crude about it. Love bombarding is very typical of the narcissist. It is its form of manipulation, and it can be downright cruel in reality.

You will feel like the most important person in someone's world. You will go along with what they say hook, line, and sinker because you truly trust in what they say. Once this person has you there, they can easily force their will and beliefs onto you. Fighting against this is extremely difficult for some people.

Becoming solid in your belief system will make it more difficult for someone to pray on your emotions. Another way to combat this dark tendency is to work on really knowing yourself. When you spend the time meditating, self-actualizing, and maintaining control of yourself, it is much easier to fend off attacks on your emotions.

When someone manipulates your emotions, it can have a detrimental impact on the rest of your life. Narcissists and Psychopaths cannot often have true feelings. They are shut off, in a way. So, them playing with yours is a simple way to gain control of you and the situation they are in. Practicing NLP's art can also give you signs of when these types of people are trying to harm you.

Gut feelings and red flags should be paid attention to. Naturally, we have instincts, and sometimes something just feels off from the beginning. Maybe you meet someone, and they seem just a little too perfect, or you just feel a bit uncomfortable around them, don't disregard these thoughts and feelings. We are wired to sense danger. This is not just the physical danger that we sense but also an emotional and mental danger. The phrase "go with your gut" is a good one that can help you avoid unpleasant situations.

Chapter 17. Brainwashing

Brainwashing is a particular form of manipulation or control over someone else used through very specific means. Usually, when you use brainwashing, you refer to a particular pattern typically used in hostage situations to try to get the other person to give in to control. Brainwashing most often occurs in the context of trying to get someone else to conform to something new. The purpose of brainwashing comes right down to thought reform—when it is used, the entire purpose is to get compliance and reeducation to encourage someone to become someone they are not. We will also take a look at the most common steps to going through the process.

Defining Brainwashing

Perhaps the first reported source of brainwashing was recorded during the Korean War. During this time, it is said that several American prisoners of war were held in prison camps and were brainwashed into believing that they had engaged in germ warfare and pledged allegiance to communism. When this happened, they were effectively stripped of their identities, forced to comply, and denounced everything that they had known of their past lives. They had their thoughts rewritten through coercion and threat.

Brainwashing is a form of influence designed to be invasive and forceful to break down others' minds. They eventually comply in hopes of protecting themselves from being hurt worse. It becomes self-preservation to do whatever they are told to do to protect themselves. As a result, they are willing to take on complex personas that are entirely dictated by the captors.

The Science of Brainwashing

Brainwashing is believed to work because the agent, that is to say, the person doing the brainwashing, is gaining complete and utter control over the target. This person is being brainwashed in the first place. This makes it so that the agent has complete power over everything and anything related to the individual. The agent gets to determine when needs can be met and how they are. Over time, the result is a systematic destruction of everything that goes into making that person who they are. Over time, because they can't meet their needs, they feel like their identities are destroyed to the point of no longer being viable. Over time, through torture, coercion, and control, brainwashing can occur. Typically, however, it should be noted that the individual's old identity can be returned over time. After leaving the dangerous situation, it is possible, with therapy, for the old identity to be returned.

Using Brainwashing

When brainwashing happens, it is usually done through several steps designed to be as effective as possible. These steps are brutal, but that is the entire purpose of it all. It is designed to be brutal so that it can have its intended effect. Let's go over the steps that go into this method now.

1. Assault on identity: The first step is designed to help to break down the self. It is an assault on your direct identification. It is designed to make you feel like you are not who you are. Typically, in the actual context, the agent will deny everything. They will directly contradict anything that the individual may say is true. As this happens, the individual is repeatedly attacked to the point of exhaustion and eventually even giving in to what the other person said.

2. Guilt: The individual has to be made to feel guilty. This is done so that the individual is more likely to give up his or her identity. When that entire identity is wrapped up in guilt, it is easier to get rid of it and pretend that it is not there than it is to do anything else. By rejecting the identity entirely, the individual is even closer to being brainwashed.

3. Self-betrayal: The stage in which the agent gets the target to agree with what has been said. The agent wants the target to recognize that he or she is bad and that it is time to denounce who they once were. They need to feel like they were wrong to have the opinions that they can do better.

4. Breaking point: That betrayal culminates in what is known as the breaking point—the point at which the individual just cannot cope any longer. At this point, the target goes through what is commonly referred to as a nervous breakdown—sobbing, depression, and generally just not coping well. They may be in the middle of a psychotic episode or may have other problems going on as well. They believe that all hope is lost, and that is the key to the whole process.

5. Leniency: When all seems beyond help, that is when the agent can get in and take control. Usually, with a small kindness—offering a bit of leniency or otherwise offering a drink of water, and that small kindness is enough to make the individual feel indebted.

6. The compulsion to confess: At this point, the target realizes that they have hope. All is not lost, and they can do what it will take to protect themselves. So, what they do is they confess. They want to try to channel and relieve their stress and guilt, so they confess.

7. **Channeling the guilt**: At this point, the target assumes that they are just wrong. The target assumes that they are wrong for some reason, and want to get rid of that sense—which gets connected to their guilt. They wrap all of their guilt about identity together to release it.

8. **Releasing the guilt**: The target realizes the problem is not with him or her, but rather with the guilt and beliefs. They do not have to be permanently bad or problematic—they can get better and do better to release the pain and escape. So, they do this through confessions.

9. **Progress toward harmony:** At this point, the target can begin making a move toward what they perceive as salvation or goodness—they can rebuild themselves to be good. In doing so, in deciding to assimilate and comply, they can make the abuse stop. In denouncing the past, the target can begin choosing the new belief system, making a conscious choice to assimilate and comply. As a result, they conclude that this new identity is reliable and safe, and they follow it.

10. **Final confession**: Finally, the new life is clung to. All old beliefs are rejected, and the individual pledges allegiance to the new life instead.

Chapter 18. Brainwashing Technique

While we are focusing more on the dark psychology that comes with manipulation, you will find examples of manipulation that can occur in our daily lives. Often we don't think that we are doing it at all. We think of manipulation to get what we want from other people, but sometimes we do it to save others' feelings. For instance, how many times have you lied to someone to let them know they looked good in something, even though you didn't think so. You did this to spare their feelings, whether they are a family member or a close friend!

Even though the point of doing this was good, you still were looking to save yourself. You didn't need to be the one who said something means about the other person and how they looked. This kind of manipulation can be seen as a good thing, though, because it was done to spare the other person's feelings in the process.

With that in mind, we will take a brief look at some of the most common manipulation techniques available to us to get what we want. You are sure to recognize at least a few of these as ones that you have used at some point or another in your life, even if you did not think of it as manipulation at the time. Some of the most common manipulation techniques that you can use includes:

Lying is something that we have all done at one point or another. We do this to confuse the other person, make sure that others believe something we want, or even get ourselves out of trouble. You may decide not to go to a party one night because you don't want to go, so you say you had something with family come up. You don't like the gift, but you smile and tell the giver that you love it. We have all used lying at one point or another, and it is considered a type of manipulation. When it comes to a dark manipulator, though, lying will be done in a deliberate way that helps them succeed while ensuring that the other person gets harmed.

Another method that you can use is going to include not telling the whole story. You can imagine yourself as a teenager with this one. Your parents asked you where you were, and you say at the mall with Susan and Sally. But you leave out the fact that the boy they don't like, John, was there as well. You technically were at the mall with your friends, but you leave out the part of the story that will get you in trouble or make someone else mad.

Punishment. This is often reserved for the dark forms of manipulation, but it will still be used on occasion. Without thinking of it as manipulation, we may punish someone else when they don't do what we want. How often have we used the silent treatment against a friend or a spouse who didn't do something that we wanted?

None of us want to end up being the one to blame for something even if we were the ones who did it. We will try to get out of it by denying that anything happened at all. With another tactic known as minimizing, we may admit that something did happen. Still, we will downplay the actions and make it feel like the other person was overreacting and misreading the situation. How many occurrences have we said something we didn't mean. When the person came back to get mad at us about it, we turn it around and minimize it by saying they didn't hear the words the right way. These are probably the two methods of manipulation that we use the most to help keep us out of trouble as much as possible.

Another option that you can work with is going to be known as spinning the truth. This is something that we see all of the time with politicians. It is done so often we can usually see it happening ahead of time. The spinning of the truth will be done to turn some lousy behavior into something that doesn't seem as bad to others. This takes a bit more work to accomplish because you have to think on your feet and develop something plausible. Still, the point is to change up the story to change your perception from other people.

Even though we are not fond of it when other people do this to us, we can all admit that we have played the victim at one point or another. We know that people are more likely to feel bad when we can come up with a sob story. Maybe we try to make one particular person feel bad about how they treated us, and we will do it in front of others so that we can get what we want. Other times we may come up with a big sob story to get out of a group thing, out of late work, and more. The point here is to turn ourselves into a big victim, even though we don't deserve to have that kind of attention or that title.

Positive reinforcement is something that every parent who has wanted to keep their sanity and who has wanted to make sure that their children will follow the rules and behave will use at one point or another. This is where you will reward the behaviors you really like, the behavior you want to make sure sticks around. This can include paying a lot of attention to the target, excessive charm, and expensive presents.

Think of it this way. When your toddler is learning the rules, it is often more efficient to convince them to listen and do what they should when they get a reward. Whether it is a sticker chart, a reward of a toy or some candy or lots of praise, you will find that the more consistent you are with these, the more the toddler will continue to follow the rules. This is precisely how the idea of positive reinforcement is going to work whether you use it on a child or an adult with manipulation.

Diversion can be another way to focus on yourself and work to make sure that the other person doesn't catch on to your true meaning. How many times have you felt that someone was trying to get at your lie or coming close to figuring something you had hidden? Then you would divert the conversation away? No matter how firm they tried to get back to it, you would just push it all back at them or turn the conversation over to a new topic to get the results you wanted and keep the target away from guessing your true intentions.

Sarcasm is a technique that we have all used at one point or another, especially when we want to feel frustrated about something. We may not be able to explain things to someone else. This is going to be done in a way to make us feel more superior to other people and to lower the self-esteem of the victim. Whether we are doing it with friends as a joke or using it against someone else we want to belittle to make ourselves feel better, sarcasm is something that we are all going to be pretty familiar with.

Guilt-tripping is an excellent way for us to make sure that we can get what we want from other people. We will say things like the other person have life easy, really selfish, or don't care about us. This will make the other person feel bad and like something they did was wrong, even if they were trying to help you out with something, and they are more likely to want to try and help you some more.

How many occurrences have we all tried to use some form of flattery to get what we want from other people? This helps us get on the other person's right side, and all it takes is flattering the target praising them and using all our charm. No matter who they are, the target will be happy to get all of this praise and compliments, and it will help lower their guard a little bit in the process. This is a great one that can be used when we want to get a new job or gain up in our position when an opening happens.

As you will notice, there are many different methods of manipulation that we can use in our daily lives. It doesn't seem to matter whether we are using them just to help us get by or if we are trying to use them to help us be dark manipulators and always get what we want, no matter the consequences. How many of the methods on the list have you used at one point or another in your own life to get what you wanted?

Chapter 19. Hypnosis

What is Hypnosis

T here have been many definitions of what hypnosis is. The American Psychological Association has defined hypnosis as a cooperative interaction where the hypnotist will give suggestions to the person; he picks which he or she will respond to. Edmonton said that a person is simply but in a deep state of mind when undergoing hypnosis. Hypnosis is, therefore, when a person enters a state of mind in which a person finds himself or herself vulnerable to a hypnotist's suggestions. Hypnosis is not new to us because many people have seen it in movies, cartoons, or been to magic shows or performances where participants are told to do usual acts, and they do it. For sure, some people believe that hypnosis exists and would do anything to avoid being a victim, while others believe that its fiction.

Induction

Induction is considered as stage one of hypnosis. There are three stages in total. Induction aims to intensify the partaker's expectations of what follows after, explaining the role they will be playing, seeking their attention, and any other steps needed during this stage. There are many methods used by hypnotists to induce a participant to hypnosis. One of them is the "Braidism" technique, which requires a hypnotist to follow a few steps. This technique is named after James Braid. The first step would be to find a bright object and hold it in your left hand and specifically between the middle, fore, and thumb fingers.

The object should be placed where the participant will fix their stare and maintain the stare. This position would be above the forehead. It is always crucial that the hypnotist remind the partaker to keep their eyes on the object. If the participant wonders away from the object, the process will not work. The participant should be focused entirely on the item. The participant's eyes will begin to dilate, and the participant will start to have a wavy motion. A hypnotist will know that his participant is in a trance when the participant involuntarily closes his or her eyelids when the middle and forefingers of the right hand are carried from the eyes to the object. When this does not happen, the participant begins again, guiding that their eyes are close when the fingers are used in a similar motion. Therefore, this puts the participant in an altered state of mind. He or she is said to be hypnotized. The induction technique has been considered not to be necessary for every case. Research had shown that this stage is not as important as already known when it came to the induction technique's effects. Over the years, there have been variations in the once original hypnotic induction technique, while others have preferred to use other alternatives. James Braid's innovation of this technique still stands out.

Suggestion

After Induction, this follows the suggestion stage. James Braid left out the word suggestion when he first defined hypnosis. However, he described this stage as attempting to draw the partaker's conscious mind to focus on one central idea. James Braid would start by minimizing the functions of different parts of the partaker's body. He would then emphasize using verbal and non-verbal suggestions to get the partaker into a hypnotic state. Hippolyte Bernheim also shifted from the physical form of the partaker. This well-known hypnotist described hypnosis as the Induction of a particular physical condition, which increases one's susceptibility to the participant's suggestions. Suggestions can be verbal or one that doesn't involve speech. Modern hypnotist uses a different form of suggestions that include non-verbal cues, direct verbal suggestions, metaphors, and insinuations. Non-verbal suggestions that may be used include changing the tone, mental imagery, and physical manipulation. Mental imagery can take two forms. One consists of those that are delivered with permission and those that are done none the less and are more authoritarian.

When discussing hypnosis, it would be wise if one would be able to distinguish between the conscious mind and the unconscious mind. While using suggestions, most hypnosis will try and trigger the conscious mind other than the unconscious mind. In contrast, other hypnotists will view it as a way of communicating with the unconscious mind. Hypnotists such as Hippolyte Bernheim and James Braid, together with other great hypnotists, see it as trying to communicate with the conscious mind. This is what they believed. James Braid even defines hypnosis as the attention that is focused upon the suggestion. The idea that a hypnotist will be able to creep into your unconscious mind and order you around is next to impossible as according to those who belong to Braids school of thought. The determinant of the different conceptions about suggestions has also been the nature of the mind. Hypnotists such as Milton Erickson believe that responses given are normally through the unconscious mind. They used the case of indirect suggestions as an example. Many of the nonverbal suggestions, such as metaphors, will mask the hypnotist's true intentions from the victim's conscious mind. A form of hypnosis that is completely reliant upon the unconscious theory is a subliminal suggestion. Where the unconscious mind is left out in the hypnosis process, then this form of hypnosis would be impossible. The distinction between the two schools of thought is quite easy to decipher. The first school of thought believes that suggestions are directed at the conscious mind will use verbal suggestions.

In contrast, the second school of thought who believe that suggestions are directed at the unconscious mind will use metaphors and stories that mask their true intentions. In general, the participant will still need to draw their attention to an object or idea. This enables the hypnotist to lead the participant in the direction that the hypnotist will need to go into the hypnotic state. Once this stage of suggestion is completed and is successful, the participant will move onto the next stage.

Susceptibility

It has been shown that people are more likely to fall prey to the hypnotist tactics than others will. Therefore, it will be noted that some people can fall into hypnosis easily, and the hypnotist does not have to put so much effort. At the same time, for some, getting into the hypnotic stage may take longer and require the hypnotist to put quite the effort. While for some, even after the continued efforts of the hypnotist, they will not get into the hypnotic state. Research has shown where a person has reached the hypnotic state at some point in their lives. They will likely be susceptible to the hypnotist's suggestions, and those who have not been hypnotized, or it has always been difficult for them to reach that state. It will be likely that they may never be able to get that hypnotic state.

Different models have been established to determine the susceptibility of partakers to hypnosis. Research done by Deirdre Barrett showed that there are two types of subjects that considered being more susceptible to hypnosis and its effects. The two subjects consist of the group of dissociates and fantasizers. Fantasizers can easily block out the stimuli from reality without the specific use of hypnosis. They daydream a lot and also spent their childhood believing in the existence of imaginary friends. Dissociates are persons who have scarred childhoods. They have experienced trauma or child abuse and found ways to put away the past and become numb. If a person belongs to this group finds him or herself daydreaming, it will be associated in terms of being blank and fantasizing. These two groups will have the highest rates of being hypnotized.

Types of Hypnosis

A hypnotist can use different types of hypnosis as a participant. Each of them will use different ways and will help with certain issues. Some types of hypnosis will assist in weight loss, while others will help a participant relax.

Traditional hypnosis

This type of hypnosis is very popular and used by hypnotists. It works by the hypnotist, making suggestions to the participant's unconscious mind. The participant who is likely to be hypnotized by this does what he is told and does not ask many or frequent questions. If one was to self-hypnotize themselves, they would do this by using traditional hypnosis. As we have said, this type of hypnosis is very popular, and this could be attributed to it not requiring much skill, and it is not technical. The hypnotist will just have the right words and just tell the participant what to do. This might pose a problem to the hypnotist where the participant is a critical thinker and can analyze a given situation.

Neuro-Linguistic Programming (NLP)

This type of hypnosis gives the hypnotist wide criteria for the methods they can use in hypnosis. The hypnotist can save time during the process as the hypnotist will just use the same thought patterns to create the problem in the participant. For example, if it is stress, the same thought pattern causing this stress will be used to counter the stress.

NLP Anchoring

To understand how anchoring works, think of a particular scent. The first time you had that scent, you were going through some feeling in which the unconscious mind attached these feelings to that scent. Through this, the scent will become the anchor for those particular feelings. Every time you heard the scent, those feelings come rushing back, triggered by the unconscious mind. This type of NLP has been useful to hypnotists in the process of hypnosis. If you won a prize or some money, for example, the hypnotist will try and recreate those feelings you had when you won the prize. While recreating these feelings, the hypnotist will ensure the participant does an action during this process. Each time the subject does the said action, they will be reminded of those feelings.

This type of NLP can motivate a person to accomplish their goals, for example, if they are trying to be healthier or lose weight. The hypnotist will create a positive anchor that is in line with the mental image of the participant. The mental picture will be that of a sexy slim body. This image will be used as the motivator to start losing weight.

NLP Flash

This technique should only be done by a certified professional because it is considered very powerful and used to alter thoughts and emotions around the participant's unconscious mind. It is deemed to be helpful to persons who experience chronic stress or are addicted to a substance. Here is what the hypnotist will do; he or she is addicted to a substance instead of it, causing some feelings of happiness the act will now cause feelings of pain.

Where the person had chronic stress, the cat will bring a sense of relaxation. Those addicted to substances such as cigarettes and alcohol will now feel pain when they take these substances, which can effectively help them get over their addiction.

Chapter 20. Hypnosis Techniques

O nce you have mastered the process of hypnosis that can often be called the long process, you can begin to use another powerful form of hypnosis to your advantage, instant hypnosis. These techniques play with the basics of the mind and what can happen to everyone from time to time daily. Have you ever gazed out of the window and simply watched the rain come down? What about listening to music that makes you feel soothed and relaxed? Maybe watching a favorite movie or television show, and you just feel yourself tune out. Often when this happens, you may not even notice that your brain has checked out. You're comfortable, relaxed, and completely absorbed in what you are doing. It happens every day and has three characteristics that are telltale signs.

1. Increased focus and concentration.

2. Increased relaxation of the body.

3. Increased access to the subconscious mind.

Hypnosis simply uses this natural state of things to put your subject into that state of mind as quickly as possible.

The Handshake Technique

This technique requires that you and the subject have some trust between you. As you will reach out your hand to shake with and then pull sharply towards yourself, you will forcefully, but calming say the word sleep as you do this. If you don't have a little trust built between you, this could just as easily backfire and make the subject tense when you pull them in. How does this technique work so easily? It works by using two different methods of inducing hypnosis: moving the subject off balance, so the brain does not have time to compute a response and giving the forceful suggestion of sleep, which seems like a good idea to the brain. People are far more suggestive than they think, and that is how this simple but powerful instant technique can work.

Falling Backward Method Technique

This form of instant hypnosis again works in the process of putting someone off balance and giving them a suggestion to follow. Instead of pulling them forward towards you, however, the subject will tip slightly backward. By following simple steps, this process can put your subject under in less than a minute:

Step 1: Ask your subject to stand with their feet together and their arms hanging loosely at the side. As they get into a position to explain what you will be doing with them step by step to know what is coming next, you will let them also know this will test their relaxation reflexes.

Step2: Move to stand directly behind your subject and place both hands on their shoulders.

Stand close enough to control them as they fall, but not close enough so that they will fall directly on you. Control the fall but don't take too much weight.

Place one foot in front of the other, and you will be able to keep the right balance to hold their weight as they fall back. Tell the subject this is just a trial run.

Step 3: Ask your subject to relax and explain that you will pull them a few inches back but that you will not let them fall. Place a strong emphasis on this fact that you will not let them fall and ask them to stay relaxed and bend their body at the ankles only, not at the waist, knees, or anywhere else.

Step 4: With your hands still on the subject's shoulders, ask them to close their eyes and pull them back only a few inches. A space of two or three inches is sufficient. Remember not to jar of force them, but allow them to gently tip backward and then rock them forward again. Keep your hands firmly on their shoulders and stand the client upright again, ensuring they regained their balance.

Step 5: If your subject seems relaxed, move on to the next step. If not, assure the subject that they have done well, and repeat the earlier step again to make certain the subject knows what to expect. You may find that certain nervous subjects might require several attempts before they're fully comfortable.

Step 6: After having them fall back, you can sit them down and use a short and brief deepening technique to make sure they are deep in hypnosis. This is usually done simply using phrases such as "move deeper and deeper into hypnosis, relax" repeat this as needed to make sure that your subject is deep into hypnosis.

The Eye Test

To confirm for both you and the subject that a state of hypnosis has been reached with an instant technique, you want to use this simple process. With your subject comfortable and sitting, follow this process:

Step 1: "You feel your eyes are very heavy and completely relaxed. Each muscle around them is now relaxed. This makes your eyelids very heavy."

Step 2: "On the count of three and not before, I will ask you to open your eyes. When I ask this, you will not be able to. You are so completely relaxed that your eyelids are too heavy. You will not be able to open your eyes because your eyelids are so heavy, and you are so relaxed that you will not even try to open them."

Step 3: "Your eyelids are closed. Heavy. Sealed shut, and you can't open them."

Step 4: "One. Your eyes are closed; your eyelids are heavy. You can't open them, not even if you try. You simply can't open them. They are too heavy, so very heavy."

Step 5: "Two. You cannot open your eyes."

Step 6: "Three. Your eyes are tightly closed. Try opening them. You cannot open them, right? Your eyelids are too heavy. Stop trying, just simply relax your eyes again, no more trying to open them. As go your eyes, so you should go your body. Relax."

When you are doing this process, you do not allow your subject to try opening their eyes for more than a second or two. If you give them too much time, they will eventually be able to force their eyes open, and once they have done that, they will come out of hypnosis. If they can open their eyes right away without any effort, they have not been put under, and you will have to start again. If this does occur and open their eyes, simply tell them it's okay and that their eyes were not relaxed enough, so you will begin again. Remember to keep a festive air.

Relaxation Technique

Therapists usually ask you to make yourself feel at home and be comfy during an introduction meeting. They may even provide you with a soft couch to lay on. Why? Are they just being courteous? The truth is, it's more than that. Therapists use relaxation as a common method to induce hypnosis. If you are relaxed, you will likely fall into a trance quicker, and your mind becomes more open to accepting suggestions. Listed are some of the usual methods to promote relaxation:

- Be comfortable.

- Lay down.

- In your head, start to count down.

- Control your breathing.

- Tense your muscles and then relax.

- Speak in a calm, soft tone.

Handshake Technique

The father of hypnotherapy, Milton Erickson, became famous for using a handshake technique to get a person into a hypnotic trance. Handshake is a common greeting, but in hypnosis, it can be more than just a gesture. Hypnotists do not just shake hands in a normal way. They interrupt the subject's mind by grabbing his wrist or pulling him forward to break the balance. Because the pattern established by the subject's mind was interrupted, the client's subconscious mind will suddenly be open to suggestions.

Eyes Cues Technique

The brain has two spheres – the conscious and creative side (right) and the practical and subconscious side (left). When we are in a conversation with someone, we look for feedback to know how they feel or react to what we say. Watch your subject's eyes. Are they looking to the right? Or are they looking to the left? Remember, when they're looking to the right, that suggests that they are conscious of the current situation. If they are looking to the left, that means they are in subconscious thought.

Visualization Technique

You can use visualization to induce your subject into a hypnotic trance and make suggestions. For instance, ask your subject to visualize a room that they know very well. Instruct them to visualize each detail in that room: the windows, the smell, the lighting, the color of the wall, the texture of the floor. Then, ask them to visualize a room they do not know, such as your office. As they struggle to remember the exact details of the room they are less familiar with, they open their minds to suggestions.

Arm Levitation Technique

You can perform this by asking your subject to close their eyes. Then, ask them to notice the difference between their arms. They might say their arms are heavy or light. Subconsciously, they will enter a trance and lift their arms or make their mind believe they have lifted their arms. Either way, induction is a success.

Sudden Shock/Falling Backwards Technique

As with the handshake technique, a subject in shock can enter into a trance. You might have heard about "trust falls." The feeling of falling backward can put the body into shock. Thus, it opens the mind to accept suggestions. Of course, you must catch your subject and be very careful not to drop him/her.

Hypnotic Trigger Technique

There are several forms of hypnotic triggers. A trigger lets the subconscious remember a desired feeling or action that is suggested while under hypnosis. Here are some examples:

- Finger snap

- Clap

- Sound of ball

- Opening eyes

- Standing or sitting

Touch Technique

In this technique, the hypnotist or psychiatrist will put the subject into a relaxed state of mind. Then, gently, the hypnotist will tap the subject's hands with his/her own with slight pressure. With a pen held directly in front of the subject, they will follow it with their eyes while visualizing a perfect place in their mind. This technique needs to be repeated several times during each session. Every after the session I have with this technique, I am always relaxed and feel better.

Chapter 21. Mind Controls Hypnotism

How to Hypnotize People

T alking about any professional hypnosis instructor, they notify their clients that a successful hypnotherapist is usually confidential. Ideally, you motivate confidence in your clients with the method of 'Personality Assurance.' In other words, the clients get to the state, whereby they feel better when you are around. Of course, this is the same when you invent the method of delivering speeches to hypnotize your audience. To start with, you need to cultivate confidence in your ability when with the audience. You portray a nervous mood at the same time.

Ideally, you tend to put your client/audience in the state. They feel like you cannot find them in the room; you portray the narratives in their minds. This could be done with the ideology of focusing your attention so carefully to ensure that your words have a real effect on their perception, consciously, and unconsciously. Changing the functioning of your immune system or blood circulation tends to be done by a competent hypnotist.

A good narrator must understand the idea of you wanting to be sufficiently convincing your listeners to concentrate on what you say. This is necessary because you need them to disassociate themselves from their concerns and situations to travel to different times, places, and opportunities with you. So, at least for a while, you tend to make them understand the benefits of implementing the new ways of seeing reality.

Helping people learn new ways of responding to life, with the aim of not letting low confidence, phobias, and attention mess them up is so useful for 'Therapy hypnosis.' You concentrate your audience's attention so selectively when you speak with power that they become hypnotic rather than purely aware of the essence of their living. Therefore, this kind of education seems more profound for people.

Avoiding the Boredom Trance

However, it appears that various kinds of trances are in the crowd. You tend to hypnotize the audience by making them be in the state of leaving the room psychologically when you aren't inspiring them. Instead, the groups will try not to obey your concept and try to avoid your voice. In most cases, they begin imagining what they will do for the day, what their next social arrangements will be like, or even what they will cook for lunch. The audience/participant tends to be disassociating, but not in the ways we would like. However, it appears that the specific technique to guide your audience in the proper direction seems to be available.

Crowd Hypnosis

Professional public presenters tend to captivate the audience with thoughts and words. Also, what they will use are the anticipation, vocabulary, narrative, and initial pace. This means that implementing the ideas for their audience to act on in the future will be their ideal objective. This method tends to be very useful when it comes to hypnotizing the audience. This means that the hypnotic speakers don't give just facts. Instead, they serve the audience with an experience that will improve how they feel, think, or even behave.

Prepare Your Speech With Words That Appeal to Feelings

'Nominalization' happens to be the term in which the people who have to travel inwards to communicate with personal meanings are called. This idea helps in hypnotizing the audience. These happen to be words like mighty, lovely, devotion, wisdom, power, and so on. What's just needed is that you ensure that you align the terms with what you mean. Ideally, such correctly used terms need to contain more than mere concrete words, but words evoke feelings.

Paint Vision of Hearing Minds Through Combining Senses

We portray a paradise-like experience to someone, the moment we hypnotize them. And indeed, in pictures, words, sounds, feelings, tastes, and as well as emotions, we dream. You need to tell what you've seen, felt, heard, and tasted when you say a story about something that has happened to you when giving speeches.

Ideally, an address becomes more elegant with the implementations of this sensory appeal. For instance, "When I heard a sickening scream, I was carrying a huge bag through the mall, I turned around and saw two giant guys trying to mug an old lady who pushed them into the realm" sounds more appropriate. Compared to this, "I went to the shopping center and witnessed a serious physical conflict."

Tell All Your Stories to Hypnotize

When there are great stories to tell, tell your viewers/audience overwhelmingly, even at the moment when you're giving a talk about molecular biology.

Fascinate With Your Voice

Think about words that have significance and relevance. So, in other words, you need to speed up with your voice at times. Then sometimes slow down a bit. Perhaps, this shouldn't happen every single time to avoid getting upset. You need to reduce the speed you implement in your words when you make an argument of significance. Then, also, you can even talk to a real hypnotist calmly and on slow delivery, periodically.

Use Suddenness

We tend to go into a hypnotic spell when we're shocked or surprised, not only when we loosen up.

Humor, as it is, tends to amuse someone. So, great speakers implement the idea of using humor because it is hypnotic. There tends to be a punch on a punch line in some other perspectives, and that is because it is surprising. Mainly, the shock is often used by the hypnotists from different stages to track subjects quickly into a hypnotic state.

Be Powerful

You can create a hypnotic state for people by merely exerting power over others. Look at how people are likely to follow a person who appears to be powerful blindly. When you do this, you can get a following, and the people following you will do what you say because they want to please you and stay in your presence.

You can use this technique among your friends, family, coworkers, and any person you have a pre-existing relationship with. You want to exert your power over time so that it does not feel too aggressive. Once you notice you have followers, start small with what you are asking. They will do it without even thinking twice about it. Over time, you can ask for larger things, and you will have no trouble getting them.

Mirroring

Now, the powerful approach works for people, you know, but what about strangers? This is where mirroring comes into play. This allows you to quickly develop a rapport with someone once they see you both have someone in common. This can almost put them into a trance because they will naturally like you and want to please you since they will perceive both of you as very similar.

To successfully use this technique, pay attention to the stranger's common phrases and body language. Look at their behaviors. Exhibit these things back at them. As you continue your interaction with them, it will not take long to notice the similarities. You do not even have to lie about things you have in common. Simply mirroring their language and behaviors is enough to get them under your spell.

Use Stories

The good stories can put people into a trance-like state. Think back to when you were a kid, and your parents would read stories to you before bed. This would induce a deep state of relaxation. The same is true when you are an adult.

As you are talking to people each day, add in some anecdotes. This shows you personally and can even give you a sense of power and authority. You want people to visualize what you are saying, so use imagery to tell your story.

For example, you want a person to move something breakable because you just do not want to risk it. Do not just ask them to move it carefully. State that you do not want the vase to be dropped since it can shatter. They will visualize the vase shattering, forcing them to not only be careful when moving it, but they will volunteer to do it. They will almost see completing the task successfully as a type of personal challenge.

Lengthy Speeches

When you want to induce hypnosis on a large group, lengthy speeches are how to do it. Think about the television evangelists you have seen. They essentially use this form of hypnosis to get people to hand over thousands of dollars every time they hold a service.

When they are delivering their speech, they take a few pauses. They use varied voice tones to annunciate points and keep people completely engrossed in what they are saying. They know what their message is, and they repeat it frequently. However, they often use different phrasing, so no one in the audience ever feels like something is being forced on them.

It is not uncommon for them to tell you exactly what to do without directly telling you to do it. When you're in this type of situation, you are so enamored with the speaker that you will do just about anything they ask. They always present their lengthy speech, and then they just pass the collection basket. They do not ask you to donate because they know you will. After all, you feel dedicated to them.

You can use this technique too. You do not need an auditorium for it either. If you need something from a person or a group of people, plan out a speech. Make sure that those you are talking to feel empowered throughout the lesson. By the time you get to the end, you have already subconsciously implanted in their minds what you want. You will not need to ask for it. You will just get it.

For example, you want people to invest in your new business idea. Give them a speech about the business, about how much starting it would mean to you, and then insert a bit of a sob story about how this is your dream. Still, financially, you cannot swing it. After listening to your dramatic speech, they will feel compelled to invest.

Stacking

This is a hypnotic technique that works because you nearly overwhelm the people you are talking to. With this technique, you essentially bombard people with information. They are learning so many new things that they do not have time to sort through it. They do not feel they need to check facts because you are speaking with such authority that they automatically believe what you are saying. By the time you end your thoughts, you have essentially put them into a trance.

Cold Reading

This is something that psychics use to convince people that they can read their minds and predict their future. You will start by making a vague statement. For example, if you know a person to be shy, you will state this. You know it is accurate, and they will elaborate, giving you further information. You will use this additional information to make other predictions essentially. Once a person feels that you have this almost clairvoyant ability, they are more prone to believe anything you tell them.

Chapter 22. Dark NLP

'Neuro-Linguistic Programming' (NLP) is like a user manual for the brain that helps you communicate the unconscious mind's goals and desires to the conscious self. Imagine you are in a foreign country and craving chicken wings. You go to a restaurant to order the same, but when the food shows up, it ends up being liver stew... because of a failed communication.

Humans often fail to recognize and acknowledge their unconscious thoughts and desires because many get lost in translation to the conscious self. NLP enthusiasts often exclaim, "the conscious mind is the goal setter, and the unconscious mind is the goal-getter."

The idea of being your unconscious mind wants you to achieve everything that you desire. Still, if your conscious mind fails to receive the message, you will never set the goal to achieve those dreams.

NLP was developed using excellent therapists and communicators who had achieved great success as role models. It's a set of tools and techniques to help your master communication, both with yourself and others.

NLP is the study of the human mind combining thoughts and actions with the perception to fulfill their deepest desires. Our mind employs complex neural networks to process information and use language or auditory signals to give it meaning while storing these signals in patterns to generate and store new memories.

We can voluntarily use and apply certain tools and techniques to alter our thoughts and actions in achieving our goals. These techniques can be perceptual, behavioral, and communicative. They can be used to control our minds and those of others.

One of NLP's central ideas is that our conscious mind has a bias towards a specific sensory system called the preferred representational system (PRS). Phrases like "I hear you" or "sounds good" signal an auditory PRS, whereas a phrase like "I see you" may signal a visual PRS.

A certified therapist can identify a person's PRS and model their treatment around it. This therapeutic framework often involves rapport building, goal setting, and information gathering, among other activities.

NLP is increasingly used by individuals to promote self-enhancement, such as self-reflection, confidence, social skill development, but primarily by communication.

NLP therapy or training can be delivered in language and sensory-based interventions, using behavior modification techniques customized for individuals to better their social communication and improved confidence and self-awareness.

NLP therapists or trainers strive to make their clients understand that their view and perception of the world are directly associated with how they operate in it. The first step toward a better future is a keen understanding of their conscious self and contact with their unconscious mind.

It is paramount to first analyze and subsequently change our thoughts and behaviors that are counterproductive and block our success and healing. NLP has been successfully used to treat various mental health conditions like anxiety, phobias, stress, and even post-traumatic stress disorder.

An increasing number of practitioners are commercially applying NLP to promise improved productivity and achievement of work-oriented goals that ultimately lead to job progression.

Here are some prominently used NLP techniques.

Anchoring

Try this yourself! Think of a gesture or sensation on your body (pulling your earlobe, cracking your knuckles, touching your forehead), and associating it with any desired positive emotional response (happiness, confidence, calmness, etc.), recalling and reliving the memory when you experience those emotions.

Content Reframing

This NLP technique is best suited to combat negative thoughts and feelings. With these visualization techniques, you can alter your mind to think differently about situations where you feel threatened or underpowered.

Rapport Building

Rapport is the art of generating empathy in others by pacing and mirroring their verbal and nonverbal behaviors. People like other people who they think are similar to themselves.

When you can subtly mirror the other person, their brain will fire off "mirror neurons" or "pleasure sensors" in their brains, making them feel a sense of liking for you.

Dissociation

The NLP technique of dissociation guides you in severing the link between negative emotions and the associated trigger. For instance, certain words or phrases may instantly bring back bad memories and make you feel stressed or depressed. If you can successfully identify those triggers and make an effort to detach those negative feelings, you are one step closer to healing and empowering yourself.

Future Pacing

The NLP technique of leading the subject to a future state and rehearsing the potential future outcomes to achieve the desired result automatically is called future pacing. It's a type of visualization technique or mental imagery used to anchor a change or resource to future situations by imagining and virtually experiencing those situations.

Influence and Persuasion

This is the most ambivalent NLP technique and houses a gray area between dark psychology and psychotherapy.

NLP is primarily focused on eliminating negative emotions, curbing bad habits, and resolving conflicts. Another aspect of NLP deals with ethically influencing and persuading others. Now pay attention to the word ETHICAL here.

How to Use NLP as a Useful Tool to Manipulate?

Your intentions are the only North Star in a dark and lonely ocean. It is the only thing that sets NLP apart from manipulation by serving as a useful tool to remember the actual purpose of using NLP. Studies show that your brain subtly works towards achieving them when innately aware of your goals, even when you aren't actively thinking about it. It is known as "diffused thinking" when you allow your mind to wander freely, making connections randomly. It's a process that encompasses all parts of the brain and is commonly used to solve problems and difficult concepts.

The true motive can sit undisturbed, deep in your subconscious, while your brain works around it, trying to develop ways and plans to achieve it. NLP is a set of skills that allows you as the user to be in control of your own conscious and unconscious mind.

However, that doesn't mean that NLP is unsuccessful if the user's intentions are immoral. It is possible to imbue those habits known to be practiced by historically unsavory characters, such as criminals and terrorists; thus, the patient can be fashioned into the next revolutionary terrorist who ushers in a new era completely reinvents modern violence as we know it. This is an example of the more extreme cases. Subtler manipulation, the kind that may not make headlines and morning news, can be equally deadly.

For example, consider this hypothetical scenario between two rival law firms competing for the same large client. Law firm A plans to manipulate the client's choice by presenting their rival law firm in a bad light. This is done by hiring a programmer to sit in on the regular therapy sessions of law firm B's top attorney and subtly twist the patient's view of his/her relationship with their spouse, thereby planting subconscious suggestions of problems in the relationship that do not exist. This technique would fall under the category of manipulation in court, with or without NLP.

Another instance of manipulation your brain doesn't commonly recognize because humans are sympathetic creatures is the emotional manipulation done by beggars. Though there is a percentage of 'honest' beggars, who are truly homeless and struggling to survive, there is a great majority of those whose trade is begging.

It is quite popular in the South Asian region, and the manipulators often don patchy clothes and have dirty faces. They use words and behaviors to play on the emotions to convince people that they need money. Many even go the extra mile and hire children for the day, just to rub it in. The manipulation is done so well that whether they have trained themselves in NLP techniques or not, they are very good at it.

On the other hand, NLP programmers hired to hold regular workshops in businesses (such as our hypothetical law firms, for instance) use it as a tool to help boost employee motivation, and encourage them to pick up new skill-sets that have been attributed to highly successful individuals, in a bid to improve general worker productivity and employee attitude in the company. It is a technique that has shown positive results.

Similarly, as it is used in business purposes to inspire workers, it is also commonly employed by a door-to-door salesman to sell as many products as possible and earn higher commissions.

Personal programmers work with their clients to help them repair relationships with their friends and family, rectifying and solving conflicts. NLP is also clinically utilized in curing mental illnesses like PTSD, GAD, phobias, anxieties, paranoia, and even substance abuse.

There are many more instances where NLP is employed, for good and bad, but the prevailing truth of the matter is that NLP itself is not guilty. Like any technique or product, there are users and abusers.

The thing being abused is innocent of the crime of the abuser. It's NLP abusers with evil, nefarious motives that have brought a bad name on the personal development and psychotherapy technique so well-intended by Brandler and Grinder.

Chapter 23. The Positive and Negative Aspects of Neuro Linguistic Programming

There are both positive and negative parts of neuro phonetic programming or NLP. Tragically, not many individuals have a complete comprehension of this term, even though they are dependent upon it each and ordinary. More critically, many organizations, associations, and people who realize how to control this idea, regularly do such with exploitative aims.

NLP is the investigation of how verbal correspondence impacts the human cerebrum. The words that you hear are answerable for forming your discernments, thoughts, and even your activities. This is the essential thought behind uplifting feedback. In contemplates, uplifting statements have been appeared to make significant enhancements in mentalities and practices. Neuro etymological programming characterizes why this works.

On the other hand, negative words additionally sway the individuals who hear them. Individuals who are continually encompassed by antagonistic individuals will regularly fall prey to their negative talk. Expressions of demoralization will, as a rule, cause an individual to take on a naysayer mentality. This makes it almost certain that the individual will surrender before attempting. Something else to consider is how your own words may make you stay dormant in certain life territories. You must be cautious about discussing these things on the off chance that you are attempting to create change in specific examples or practices. Your cerebrum will accept a follow up on the very words that you express.

The absolute most noteworthy experts or NLP are significant promoting and publicizing organizations. They realize that their words can shape popular suppositions and free activity. To get mass-market consideration for explicit merchandise, a significant number of these elements will make individuals partner industrialism with satisfaction. Individuals at that point start to accept that they should purchase items to feel glad.

When you have an away from how verbal correspondence influences your practices, it is critical to be progressively cautious about the words you express and the organization you keep. You can likewise play a progressively active job as an audience. Individuals who listen inactively to verbal messages are unmistakably progressively liable to being influenced by them.

When you realize what neuro phonetic programming or NLP is and how it tends to be utilized, you can become much progressively amazing in your dynamic. You will be able to begin utilizing positive words to fortify yourself and the people around you. You will furthermore turn out to be progressively capable in endeavors to prevent you or to persuade you to burn through cash on superfluous things. This is genuinely one of those occurrences in which information is power.

How Negative Thinking Can Affect Us

Negative reasoning influences us inwardly, however, genuinely. To be sure, negative considerations have genuine implications past simply the idea itself. How might you use neuro etymological programming and entrancing to break liberated from this?

137

Neuro semantic writing computer programs are methods by which you can truly be instructed to "retrain" how you think. A specialist prepared in NLP can assist you with rethinking and repeat contemplations, and think about them from an alternate perspective, so you truly start to think in various manners that are increasingly adjusted and positive - and without a doubt, progressively practical.

This is an extremely positive advance to take because so regularly, negative considerations are "outside of any relevant connection to the issue at hand" based on what is truly occurring.

Negative Thinking in Every Day Situations

Suppose, for instance, that you've been doled out a venture grinding away, and you're sure you can do it. You complete the activity, and you've done quite well. In any case, you notice one modest mistake. In a split second, you start to converse with yourself adversely, disclosing that you took care of the activity inadequately, even though the one small mistake isn't huge and won't sway on the nature of the undertaking generally. So while your supervisor is stating, "Incredible employment!" you may be stating to yourself, "No, it's most certainly not. I'm so dumb. I will lose my employment on account of that botch."

How Reasonable Is That?

A certified NLP Practitioner may challenge you with this: "All in all, your manager has advised you will lose your employment since you committed one little error?" How will you respond? You'll think, "Obviously not!" and understand that your supervisor is revealing to you that you've worked superbly. Like this, neuro etymological programming truly shows us how to retrain our musings in a progressively adjusted and positive manner, given a target assessment of the natural conditions.

Presently, I don't get this' meaning regarding how you can abstain from following this example by and large? All things considered you make a stride back and take a gander at the task with target eyes. Impartially, without that negative self-talk, you can see that genuinely, you worked superbly and committed one little error. What's more, even though you need to abstain from committing errors, they do occur.

So a good repetition of your underlying response - that you took care of the activity inadequately - may be to state, "I worked admirably and committed one little error. I will focus next time and make an effort not to commit a similar error, yet I can at present be pleased with what I did, all things being equal." You can likewise disclose to yourself that because your supervisor is content with what you did, you ought not exclusively to be glad for what you've done, however. You can be secure that your activity is protected. Truth be told, what is sensible and present and is considerably more precise as self-talk than your past explanation.

Chapter 24. Understanding Body Language

What is Body Language

We sometimes do things unconsciously, much like a nervous habit, such as tapping your foot or rubbing your hands together. Though we may not be aware that we are doing these things, others see these habits and read into them. We may be seen as nervous or agitated by others due to these unconscious behaviors that we are prone to.

At other times, we might engage in an action or pose with a specific intent consciously chosen. We can choose to turn our bodies towards someone we are busy talking to seem more attentive. Imagine your first job interview: you cautiously keep yourself from twitching, rubbing your face, or reclining. You have been made aware by various knowledgeable people such as school counselors and career guides to be aware of these interview bombs. Knowing how bad these make you seem, you learn not to engage in this form of body language.

We can lie with a written and spoken language. Usually, we lie to avoid getting into trouble. Likewise, we can also lie in our bodies. We can project a disingenuous body image and has been carefully polished to accomplish a particular appearance. I imagine that several of us have been caught in a scam at some point in time. This is an ideal example of how intelligent users of body language can manipulate it to convince us of their honesty. We get people to believe us based on what we show and not what we say.

In expressing emotions, the facial expression is essential. It combines the cheeks' movement, nose, lips, eyebrows, and eyes to show a person's various moods. Some researchers showed that body and facial expressions complement each other in interpreting emotions. Some experiments recognized the influence of body expression in identifying facial expression, which means that the brain simultaneously processes body and facial expressions.

Body postures can also detect emotions. If an individual is angry, he will try to dominate another person. His posture will show such approach tendencies. If he is fearful, his approach will be that of avoidance. He will feel submissive and weak.

Even gestures have different interpretations. For instance, if an individual folds his arms during a discussion, it's going to mean that he's unwilling to concentrate on the speaker or features a closed mind. If he crosses his arms over the opposite, it means he lacks confidence and is insecure.

Simple hand gestures show that the individual is self-assured and confident, while clenched hands can mean either angry or stressed. If he wrings his hands, it means he is anxious and nervous.

Finger gestures show the overall well-being of an individual. In some cultures, it is acceptable to point with an index finger. Handshakes also show the levels of emotion and confidence of individuals. They are popular in some cultures. In Muslim cultures, a man cannot shake or touch the hands of a woman. In Hindu cultures, a man greets a woman by keeping his hands together, like praying.

When it comes to learning how to read body language, the main goal is to determine if the person in front of you is genuine. Body language clues are incredibly crucial when deciphering someone's innermost thoughts, personality, and even intentions. In many ways, body language teaches you to become a human lie detector. Humans can be great liars, but while we may have been able to trick our mind into saying words we do not mean, we cannot trick our bodies into executing the lie flawlessly.

Reading body language is an excellent skill to have in job interviews when trying to solve a crime or resolve conflict. Being able to see beneath the surface into what is going on inside someone's mind will help you make better, more informed decisions.

What makes body language so tricky to master is deciphering body language cues within the right context. For example, when a person crosses his or her arms in front of the chest, you could construe that as negative body language, perhaps an indicator that the person is not happy to be here. However, depending on the context, it could also mean that the person feels cold, uncomfortable, or frustrated. Not accounting for a situation can lead to misreading of body language cues and a wrong conclusion.

Most people generally display a few categories of body language:

Dominant: Dominant body language comes into play when someone wants to be in command. The most standout cue for this category of body language is standing tall, with chest puffed out.

Attentive: This shows someone's interest and engagement with the conversation or situation.

Bored: A typical representation of this body language is the lack of eye contact and constant yawning.

Aggressive: An aggressive person will display threatening body language cues.

Defensive: A defensive person will look as if he or she is protecting or withholding information.

Closed Off: You can recognize a closed-off person by noticing if he or she is shutting you off by crossing his or her arms and guardedly standing farther away from you.

Open: This body language is friendly and welcoming.

Emotional: We usually display this body language when we feel heavily influenced by current feelings and typically have to change moods.

The Power of Body Language

Body language extends beyond more than just the four types. It can also be divided into positive and negative body language. Positive body language draws people towards you and creates a sense of belonging and accomplishment. This includes encouraging smiles, firm handshakes, making eye contact, facing someone with your body in a neutral position, and using an encouraging tone of voice.

Negative body language is based on avoidance. It includes turning your back on someone, not facing the speaker, looking down, using a soft and insecure tone of voice, and avoiding eye contact. When someone uses this body language tells, we begin to assume the worst about that person. We see them as being dishonest, uninvested, and disinterested.

Knowing these two forms of body language, which would you choose to look at? In all likelihood, you would prefer seeing positive body language. We want to feel acknowledged and valued during our communications with other people. Seeing someone face you, look you in the eye, speak in a clear tone without hiding their mouth, and have a natural appearance due to their open posture is very encouraging and ensures that communication can happen harmoniously and smoothly.

Yet, we often use negative body language when we feel intimidated or unsure of a situation. Being skilled at using your body language would help you achieve more favorable outcomes from your daily interactions and communications.

According to Guilbeault (2018), body language's power lies in that it can help you gain things you want, such as friends or jobs; however, it can also make you lose the things you want negative body language forms. It can cost you your job, friends, and even intimate relationships. Without even opening our mouths, we can attract or repel people.

Body language can build trust, which is the crucial ingredient in all relationships, whether for work, companionship, or intimacy. Using the power of body language, you can lead a more productive and successful life. Hence, it is well worth learning how to recognize body language and its meaning in others and ourselves.

Characteristics of Body Language

In general, body language manifests an individual's emotions, meaning another person can perceive it.

First, it is understood that the signal from the body language to the receiver can be highly complicated. An individual's body language consists of multiple body parts moving or not moving together. All must be taken into account to interpret a specific person's emotion. A specific facial expression taken out of context from the person's other bodily reactions will give an incomplete or otherwise misleading analysis of their emotions.

Another characteristic is that the projected emotion from body language is perceived automatically in a way similar to speech. This characteristic makes nonverbal interaction spontaneous. There is often little need to interpret further what an individual means with their body language.

A third characteristic is that young individuals can acquire and develop body language very easily and rapidly. Children learn what gestures and facial expressions mean from their parents, friends, and even strangers who interact with them. The ease of acquiring knowledge of body language can make children carry on specific body language into their maturity.

Deciphering Body Language

To understand and use body language, you have to learn how to read it in action and view it holistically as an overall picture of what a person is trying to communicate. If you want to begin controlling your body language, you'll have to understand how it all works together in the field as well. Somebody crossing their legs away from you could mean they are shy, it could mean that they are closed off to you, or it could just mean they need to pee desperately. To be able to read what they are feeling, you need to notice how they use the space around them, group behavioral actions into clusters (clusters are multiple body language cues placed together, so if they cross their legs away from you, cross their hands, and face in a direction away from you, it isn't looking good!), and to place them into context.

Actively Listening

Suppose you are looking at somebody's posture or trying to pick up the micro-expressions in their face that occur at one-fifth of a second. In that case, you might be closer to understanding how they feel, but you might also be ignoring something more obvious. The whole point of studying body language is to understand better what people think to build a better connection. The point isn't to make you paranoid that they are continually deceiving you. It's to make you less paranoid about what they are thinking.

Proxemics

Proxemics is a fancy word used in the body language community to mean the study of personal space and proximity. You can't indeed read someone's body language without noticing where they concern you in space.

Someone seems to be paying attention to you. They have open body language. They are even pointing themselves towards you– so they're paying attention to you, right? Well, maybe not if they're on the other side of the room and not moving any closer towards you.

When it comes to reading other people, some aspects of personal space are apparent. If someone is close, it will mean they are or are trying to be more intimate. However, with some people, especially men, there is a tendency to be territorial and to feel they have more access to your personal space than you might feel comfortable with. You can use these cues to determine if someone is aggressive, friendly, or flirtatious. By reading the rest of someone's body language, you can see if they are leaning towards you to be friendly or assertive. It is quite risky to invade other people's personal space to get an advantage over them. In general, try to avoid getting too close to someone unless they invite you to by touching you or speaking at a lower volume that requires you to lean in.

Chapter 25. Deception

What is Deception?

T he definition is a theme that usually resonates within the spectrum of dark psychology. Throughout the years, it has been defined as any particular act used by a particular manipulative individual to instill certain beliefs within the victim that are usually false or only those possessing partial truths. It is usually placed in the same category as deceit, mystification, and suffrage. Deception is not usually an easy theme to understand since it involves many different things like, for example, distractions, propaganda camouflage, and concealment. The manipulator is often able to easily control the subject's mind since the victim is often led to placing immense trust in this manipulative individual. The victims often believe in whatever the manipulator will say and might even be basing plans and shaping their world base on the things that the manipulator is feeding their subconscious mind. This strong element of trust towards the manipulator can quickly fade away once the victim realizes what is going on. Because of this very reason, a certain level of skill is needed for deployment of this theme, since only then will a manipulator be able to skillfully change the focus of suspicion towards him and onto the victim's paranoia.

In most cases, deception will often present itself in relationship settings and lead the victim to have dominant feelings of distrust and betrayal between the partners in the relationship. This usually happens because deception is a theme that violates most of the rules of most relationships, together with having a negative influence on the expectations that come with the relationship. When getting into relationships, one of the usually ordinary things is always the ease of having an honest and truthful conversation with their partner. If the then learns that one of them is beginning to show signs of deception, they might have to learn the different ways of using misdirection and distractions to pry out reliable and truthful information that they need from them. The trust would have gone into a permanent rift that will not be easy to come back from since the victim will always be questioning everything that the partner will say and do, wondering whether the story is true of fabricated. Most relationships will end as soon as the deceptive partner is found out.

As we described earlier, this form of communication relies on lies and certain omissions to make the victim believe whatever he is being led to believing by the deceptive individual. This is the case; there are five main types of deceptive tactics that are seen to exist. We shall briefly touch on each one to better understand this theme.

Concealments

Probably taking home the medal of most used type of deception, concealment is basically when the deceptive individual knowingly omits information from his often relevant and important stories to the context. They can also engage in certain behaviors that would signal to hide relevant information to the subject at that particular time. A skilled manipulator is experienced enough to know that he will have to be clever to know that it's safe not to be directly in their approach but rather insinuate the lie leading the victim to their own conclusion, which is predetermined.

Exaggeration

What can be said about this? This is where an individual, in a sense, stretches the truth a bit too much with an intended goal of leading the story towards a direction that best caters to their needs. The manipulator will make a certain scenario appear more severe than it is to avoid lying directly to their victims. This is usually done to let the victim do whatever it is they want.

Lies

This is one tactic that we, as humans, use daily for one reason or another. We are often inclined to lie as a way to avoid some form of penalty. For example, if you work in the bank and you run late because of something minor, you will be inclined to lie to your boss to keep him from cutting you lose. What then can be said to be the meaning of this? This is where an individual gives information that is all south of the actual truth. They will present this completely fabricated truth to the victim, and they will believe it.

Equivocations

This is where an individual will knowingly make a statement of a contra dictionary nature intended to lead the victim to the path of confusion on what is exactly seems to be going on. This clever tactic will allow the manipulator to save his image if he is later discovered.

Understatements

This is where an individual minimizes aspects of the truth in the particular story being told at the time. They will often approach a victim preaching how something isn't that big of a deal when it is of the utmost importance.

What drives a manipulator to the deployment of the theme of dark psychology? According to research done over the years, there are usually 3 main things that motivate an individual to use deception on others. These three motives are under the umbrella of close relationships. They include self-focused motives, relationship-focused motives, and partner-focused motives. Let's look first at the motives focused on the partner. The victim will use deception in this kind of motive to avoid harming the subject or their partner. They may also use front to protect the relationship between the victim and an outside third party, avoid worrying about something about the subject, or keep the subject's self-esteem intact. Such motivation for deception will often be seen as both relationally beneficial and socially polite.

Deception's self-focused motive. This one is not considered noble as the first one and is therefore considered more inferior to the other techniques. Rather than worrying about the victim and how they feel, the manipulator will simply think about how they feel and their self-image. The manipulator uses deception to protect or enhance their self-image in this motive. To shield the victim from criticism, embarrassment, or anger, this form of deception is used.

Finally, we shall look at the relationship-focused motive of deception. The manipulative individual will use this deception to limit any harm that could come to the relationship simply by avoiding the trauma and conflict of relationships. This form of deception sometimes helps the relationship, depending on the situation. It may be the cause of harming the relationship because it will make things more complicated. For example, if you choose to hide how you feel about supper because you don't want to get into a fight, the relationship might be helpful. On the other hand, if you have an affair and choose to keep this information to yourself, it will only complicate things in the end.

Primary Components of Deception

As much as it may be difficult to clarify which factors show clear deployment of deception, some subtle components are immediate identifiers of these themes. The victim will come to be aware of these factors only when the manipulator dispatches a direct lie. Let us now dive deep into the particulars of said components.

Disguise

The first component we shall unravel is that of disguises. What usually goes on here is that the manipulator works tirelessly until he successfully creates the impression of being someone they are not. Manipulators often resort to this tactic if they want to hide something about them so deep that no one ever finds out. This could be a dark secret or just something as harmful as someone's name. This component's popular belief is that it is simply a change of clothes, just like in the moves. However, it goes far beyond this in that it also involves a complete change of one's persona. Having a rough idea of how discuses work, let us look at a few examples of how it can be used in the process of deception.

The first instance is where the manipulator changes himself to another person so as not to be discovered. An individual will do this with a view to maybe be able to get back into a particular crowd of people who are not very fond of him, revamp their whole personality to make someone like them, or further their own goals. In some instances, disguise may be used to refer to the hiding of one's true nature in the hopes of maybe hiding the effect that appears to be unpopular with that proposal. Disguises usually have adverse effects because it is generally hiding one's true intentions for a victim. When information is withheld in this fashion, it often clouds the victim's judgment. The victim ends up having the feeling of being in control of their decisions when they have been swayed towards the directions' manipulator. This is seen mainly in a political setting.

Camouflage

This is where individual works tirelessly to hide the truth in one way or another, leaving his victim clueless as to what exactly is going on. This is characterized by the manipulator's use of half-truths when divulging certain information to his victim. The victim will only be aware that camouflage has taken place when the actual truths are brought to light. A skilled manipulator with a lot of experience using camouflage is more likely to bra undetected in performing certain actions.

Simulation

The third component of deception is what is commonly referred to as simulation. This is simply the process where the victim is shown continuously subject matter that is false in every way. Further on, we get to see that simulation consists of 3 other techniques that can be used. They are mimicry, distraction, and fabrication.

Fabrication is when the manipulator takes something found in actual reality and chafes it to become this completely different thing. The manipulator will seek to either give detailed events that never happened or add some exaggerations that either make it sound better or worse than it sounds. The core of their story, however, is usually true. If the teacher gives them a bad grade, these manipulators may further the story by stating that they were given the bad results on purpose. The reality is that the manipulator did not study for the test hence his bad grade.

Mimicry is another tool that manipulators use when deploying these tactics of deception. The manipulator here usually portrays a persona that is quite close to their own, but not their own. They may present an idea similar to someone else's and give him credit for thinking about it first. This form of stimulation may be able to take pace through visual and auditory stimuli.

The last tool we shall look at is that of distraction as another form of simulation in deception. This is where the manipulator tries to get the victim only to focus their attention on everything else but the truth. How is this usually done? This is generally achieved through baiting or the offering of something more tempting than the reality itself.

Chapter 26. Dark Cognitive Behavioral Therapy

"A small behavioral change can also lead to embracing a wider checklist of healthier choices" - Chuck Norris.

What is Dark CBT?

To understand Dark CBT, we first must realize the necessary cognitive behavioral therapy and its approach to mental health and healing. Dark CBT is founded on the tried and true CBT principles employed by therapists everywhere. That is why it is guaranteed to work. Learning about CBT and then applying them as you see fit to unknowing subjects makes you very powerful.

Gain a thorough understanding of how to use CBT and maybe even use it upon yourself for practice. From there, you can begin leveraging Dark CBT as a clandestine healing method or weapon on those around you.

History of CBT

CBT was first developed by a psychologist named Aaron Beck in the 1960s. Beck noticed that his patients had internal monologues, where they spoke to themselves in the privacy of their minds.

Beck began to have his patients analyze their automatic thoughts and report them. As his patients became more conscious of their ideas, they realized how these thoughts could make or break their success. Some thoughts made them make poor decisions or drew them to untrue assumptions that made them feel bad for no reason. Other studies helped them overcome problems and feel better about themselves. By gaining awareness of their thoughts by reporting them verbally to Beck or writing them down throughout the day, his patients were able to gain more control over their thinking.

In time, Beck was able to teach his patients to harness their thoughts and become more self-aware. He taught them to think differently to feel better. He noticed that changes in thinking led to changes in behavior and emotions. Correcting flawed thinking was what helped his patients heal faster.

Since Beck's initial observation, CBT has grown by leaps and bounds. It is now better understood and has become a significant part of psychotherapy. All therapists are aware of CBT, and most therapists employ it to some degree in their practice. There are many forms of CBT, but they all have the same premise and the same goal, putting them under the enormous Cognitive Behavioral Therapy umbrella.

Now we have developed Dark CBT. Dark CBT operates on the same principles as CBT. However, it is more clandestine. Rather than using CBT on yourself or a willing psychotherapy patient, Dark CBT is something you can use on anyone without their awareness. You can apply CBT concepts to change someone's thinking to suit your needs. You can also use it on yourself, emphasizing becoming successful and achieving what you want in life. Dark CBT goes beyond simple healing and instead gives you the power to shape your life and your relationships as you desire.

Your interest in using Dark CBT may be purely altruistic, as you seek to help others who won't help themselves. Or you may have a more nefarious interest in using it to get your way and to manipulate others. How you use Dark CBT is up to you entirely, but the wealth of opportunity that Dark CBT provides you with is astounding.

Dark CBT is a relatively new method. It has not been applied to many study groups or researched extensively. Therefore, there is room for growth and experimentation in Dark CBT. You may find new applications or new ways of performing Dark CBT that is already unheard of. This is a new field that you can certainly expand and make your own. Supplement your Dark CBT with simple CBT methods and experiment with trial and error. You may just find your type of therapy that works well for you, based on the incredible techniques included and in basic CBT.

Why Use CBT?

There has been much success using CBT to treat difficulties in people's lives, ranging from depression to alcoholism to drug dependency to relationship problems. It can help people quit bad habits and feel better about themselves. It can also help people learn how to cope with their mental ailments to feel better. Even people who are not mentally ill can benefit from using CBT thought processes to tackle challenging problems in their lives, such as marriage difficulties, difficulties with communication, anger management issues, and even financial struggles.

The great thing about CBT is that it is possible to use on yourself. With the help of a CBT journal, you can document your thoughts and emotional reactions to events in your life or emotional wounds you are trying to overcome, or bad habits you are trying to break free of. Then, you ask yourself questions that lead you to change how you look at the situation, wound, or habit. You write down your new mental approach and new emotions now that you are using different thinking. You will notice a drastic improvement in your feelings and outlook on life. Suddenly, you won't have so many difficulties in life, and your problems will become so easy to solve that they will practically disappear before your eyes.

Dark CBT is incredibly useful for two reasons. The first is that Dark CBT is focused on personal gains and success. Rather than just healing your annoying thinking habits, you learn to become a massive success at anything that you wish. You can make yourself invincible if you teach yourself to believe that you are capable of anything. You can also create a monster by teaching someone else to feel the same way.

The second is that Dark CBT is sneaky. So even if someone is not interested in changing his thinking, you can still use Dark CBT on him to achieve the results that you desire. You will enjoy success, and he won't even know what has happened to him. You can fix people who refuse to get help or change people who stand in your way. No one will guess what you are doing. You simply seem to be an interested friend or loved one, trying to help someone think more realistically or positively.

What Separates Dark CBT From Regular CBT?

We already talked about this a little bit. But we want to stress that Dark CBT is the same as regular CBT. Its uses and applications are a bit different, however. That is the only thing that separates the two types of CBT.

Regular CBT is used in therapy or by individuals who are actively interested in changing their thinking. People use CBT knowingly and willingly. Their desire to change can make CBT very useful. You will find that you can use CBT to correct your problems, or you can visit a therapist who will set goals for you and help you adjust your thinking. The entire process is transparent and known to all parties.

Dark CBT is more opaque, hidden by a veil of deception. The subject of Dark CBT most likely is not aware of what is going on. Dark CBT is significant because it is subliminal, and it makes someone think that there is something wrong with him so that he strives to change it. You never reveal that you are the therapist here. You are also never asked to perform Dark CBT on anyone. This can be unethical, but again, you are using Dark CBT at your own risk.

Dark CBT is not evil in and of itself. It can be used for evil, but that is your call. The altruistic and positive applications of Dark CBT can be especially useful if you choose to make someone better through Dark CBT. You can help people who can't help themselves and who are resistant to getting help. You also create your success, furthering your own goals, and getting ahead in life. You don't have to become a monster and use Dark CBT to hurt people to gain from it. Using Dark CBT as a way to help others can improve your own life because it will heal your relationships and make people like you more. People will associate you with feeling better and liking themselves more, so they will want to spend more time around you. And everyone knows that being liked by people gets you what you want.

Even if you do choose to use the darker applications for Dark CBT, you won't ever get caught. People will not be aware of what you are doing. Therefore, you won't hurt your subjects or destroy relationships. You also won't get into trouble because you are not doing anything illegal.

Chapter 27. The Art Of Using Your Mind to Succeed

M any people want to learn about dark psychology because they want to do better in their careers. They aren't content working the job they already have: they want to prove themselves capable of more.

But somewhere along the way, we figure out the truth: that getting ahead in our careers isn't necessarily a matter of skill but manipulation and persuasion. As you know, dark psychology is the best and most legitimate way to learn these skills, and now it's time to learn how to use them specifically in a work setting.

We have to think in a more challenging way about how we interact with our co-workers. For instance, let's say we have a female early 20-something analyst amid a post-graduation down-cycle who has encountered many challenges both professionally and personally since starting work a few years ago.

She frequently finds herself wanting to connect with people who are perceived to be more advanced in their careers or whose interests are different from her own. Identifying why you are attracted to certain people is a valuable skill for early-career practitioners. It likely contributes to her success as an analyst. If she wants to get ahead, she should follow along with all the directions in these pages, where we speak to dark psychology in the workplace directly.

Personality is an incredibly crucial subject for the workplace context because it is an environment where you have to interact with many different kinds of people, many of whom—you will soon find out—you don't know that well as people.

Dark psychology is broader than neurolinguistics programming, but NLP is where all of our tools and techniques of in-depth communication and manipulation come from. NLP is where the three significant steps of manipulation and mind control originate from:

- Establish your state control and perceptual sharpness.

- Imitate the unconscious cues of communication of your subject so that they incorporate you into their mind.

- Use one of the techniques.

People continuously think without even realizing it because most thought is unconscious. NLP is how we take advantage of most studies' cold nature to tell people's minds to change the structure before they even know it.

NLP's topic is vital for discussing workplace personalities because NLP has five main categories for the kinds of characters' people have. In the jargon of NLP, these "personalities" are actually called metaprograms. You would do well to identify the important people at your workplace within these metaprograms. Take advantage of your perceptual sharpness to ascertain this information.

As we have told you before, getting information about the subject is everything. But it is also true that our brains need to sort all the information we get into categories to understand the world better. These metaprograms do that job for you.

Metaprograms are more useful than personalities because they are more objective. They also focus on the motivations people have and how they use logic rather than their mannerisms or less essential behavior patterns. Metaprograms do not merely describe how much you like attention or how nervous or relaxed you are. You may notice some aspects of each metaprogram that overlap with these traits. Still, metaprograms are more specific than these less useful terms.

These NLP-styled personalities are not only a way for you to get more information about your co-workers. Remember the second step of NLP's mind-reading and manipulation: you have to imitate the communications cues the subject shows you. When you do this, you make them unconsciously see you as being like themselves. That means if you take on the traits of your co-worker's metaprogram, you make it easier for you to succeed in this step.

The last thing for you to know about metaprograms, in general, is that they are sorted in dichotomies. A dichotomy is a contrast between two items that are different. But while you should choose just one from each dichotomy in each metaprogram, you must remember that people are not as simple as being A or B. Any time we have a dichotomy—in any situation—picking one of the two is just a category you can use to simplify things and think of them differently. But you should not think of them as being always or exclusively one of the two. People are much more complicated than this.

Our first metaprogram is between the dichotomy of options and procedures. People who are on the options metaprogram don't like being limited or being told what to do. They want as much freedom as possible, and they like to think about things from a general perspective rather than getting in the weeds. On the other hand, people on procedures need to understand every small detail whenever they get into something new. Procedures people hate the feeling that they are missing something. When an element is skipped, they fear they are missing something important.

The second metaprogram is external and internal. This metaprogram is concerned with people's incentives. External people want to be told by others when they do good work, and they want to be notified when they do bad work, too. Internal people don't want to get outside opinions about their work, though. They feel they know when their work is good or not, and hearing what other people think is just a bother.

The third dichotomy in metaprograms is proactive and reactive. These metaprograms describe how someone deals with the future. Reactive people look at a calendar and are always thinking about how the work they are doing. Now fits into the picture of all of their work. This can be a hindrance because they believe so much about planning to lose sight of what they are trying to do right now. Proactive people, on the other hand, hate thinking about the future or planning ahead. They only care about the here and now.

Our second-to-last is toward and away. This metaprogram is about goals and deterrents. All of us have things we look forward to in the future, but toward people are chiefly concerned about their goals, and they don't look behind them at all. Away people are the exact opposite of this. They can have issues looking ahead because they spend so much time thinking about what is behind them.

Finally, we have sameness and difference. Sameness people have a love for familiarity: they spend their time around things they already know. Things they don't know will make them fearful, so these people avoid them at all costs. On the other hand, different people are always craving new experiences to have new people meet, fresh foods to eat, etc. If there is something they haven't experience yet, different people want to share it.

These are the five significant dichotomies in metaprograms. Whoever the co-worker is who you want to use our dark psychology tricks on will want to sort them into these metaprograms. Now, when you use the Aristotelian technique of envisioning the future, you have a more objective stand-in for the person you will interact with.

When we imagine someone in our heads, it isn't always accurate to how they are. NLP's metaprograms are useful because they make us think carefully about our subject's kind of person.

Metaprograms are particularly useful for the work environment because they force us to think about the people we work with more objectively. When you do Step 1 and prepare to get into the co-worker's mind with Step 2, you can use these metaprograms to paint a fuller picture of who you will use dark psychology on.

Since these are often just people we interact with exclusively in work environments, we can be surprised by how little we might know about them from a metaprogram standpoint. If you are honest with yourself as you sort them into these dichotomies, you might realize you don't know very much about them at all. When this turns out to be the case, don't just go along with the dark psychology technique anyway. There is no point in doing this when it won't always work—you can't adapt to the social cues of a person you don't even know yet.

That's why from here, you will have to do more intel-gathering on them first before you can even move on to Step 1. Step 1 can't successfully happen until you know the person and how they fit into all the metaprograms. Until you do that, you won't be able to properly imagine your interactions with them for Steps 2 and 3.

With that said, after you get to know the co-workers' metaprograms, let your senses do all the work in perceptual sharpness, use our exercises to prepare your state control, and imagine the interaction in your imagination, you are ready for Step 2.

For Steps 2 and 3, things go about the same when you are dealing with someone from your workplace. However, some techniques seem tailor-made for use in the work setting. We will go over these before moving onto our big lesson on neurolinguistics programming in psychology.

We will cover three big dark psychology techniques for the workplace before diving into the world of NLP. Social framing is a technique in which we paint a picture for the subject where adopting a particular behavior or idea will help them with social climbing.

Our social lives are one of the most important things to us as humans. That's why framing the truth about the subject's social environment is such a powerful tool for manipulating and mind-controlling people. As long as we make them believe they get a social reward for doing what we say, they will jump at the opportunity.

Executing this technique is simple. Assuming you have already mentally sorted these techniques into the proper metaprograms, controlled your state, and paid close attention to your senses.

Chapter 28. Dark Personalities

D ark psychology is not a single, universally applicable medical diagnosis that can be applied across all cases of deviant personalities. In fact, there are a wide variety of ways that dark psychology may manifest itself in someone's psychological and behavioral makeup. There is no absolute division of one deviant personality type from another. Many bizarre personalities with prominent dark psychology features may display more than one manifestation of dark psychology.

We will explore three types of dark psychology personalities. It is important to remember that although the internet has spawned a massive growth in problems resulting from dark psychology, these traits have been part of human culture since ancient times. One of the dark psychology profiles we will explore here, Machiavellianism, takes its name from a medieval politician. Another narcissism takes its name from an ancient mythological character. Together, the three dark psychology profiles talked about here—psychopathy, Machiavellianism, and narcissism— make up what is known as "the Dark Triad."

The Dark Triad Personalities

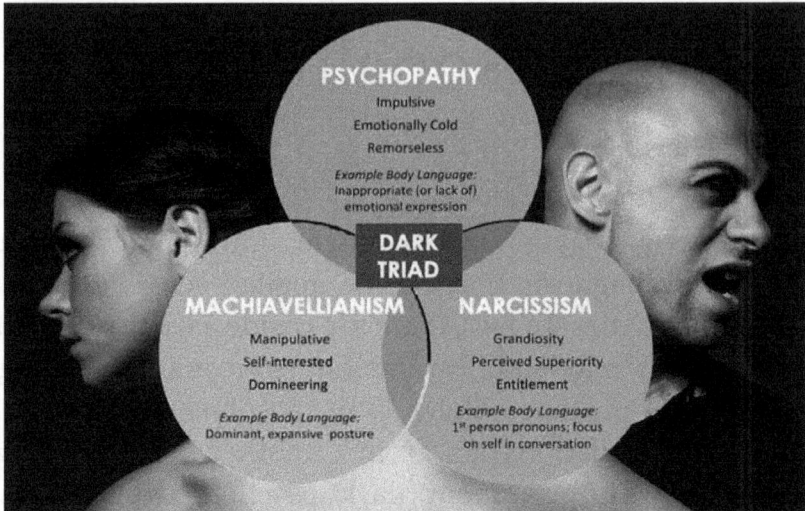

Narcissism

The term "narcissism" originates from an ancient Greek myth about Narcissus, a young man who saw his reflection in a pool of water and fell in love with the image of himself. In clinical psychology, narcissism as an illness was introduced by Sigmund Freud and has continually been included in official diagnostic manuals as a description of a specific type of psychiatric personality disorder.

In psychology, narcissism is defined as a condition characterized by an exaggerated sense of importance, an excessive need for attention, a lack of empathy, and, as a result, dysfunctional relationships. Commonly, narcissists may outwardly display a too high level of confidence. Still, this façade usually hides a very fragile ego and a high degree of sensitivity to criticism. There is often an enormous gulf between a narcissist's highly favorable view of himself or herself, the resulting expectation that others should extend to him or her favors and special treatment, and the disappointment when the results are quite negative or otherwise different. These problems can affect all areas of the narcissist's life, including personal relationships, professional relationships, and financial matters.

As part of the Dark Triad, those who exhibit traits resulting from Narcissistic Personality Disorder (NPD) may engage in relationships characterized by a lack of empathy. For example, a narcissist may demand constant comments, attention, and admiration from his or her partner but will often appear unable or unwilling to reciprocate by displaying concern or responding to their partner's circumstances, thoughts, and feelings.

Narcissists also display a sense of entitlement and expect excessive reward and recognition, but usually without ever having accomplished or achieved anything that would justify such feelings. There is also a tendency toward excessive criticism of those around him or her. Combined with heightened sensitivity when even the slightest amount of criticism is directed at him or her.

Thus, while narcissism in popular culture is often used as a pejorative term and an insult aimed at people like actors, models, and other celebrities who display high degrees of self-love and satisfaction. NPD is a psychological term that is quite distinct from merely having high self- esteem. The key to understanding this aspect of dark psychology is that the narcissist's image of himself or herself is often completely idealized, grandiose, and inflated and cannot be justified with any real, meaningful accomplishments or capacities make such claims believable. As a result of this discord between expectation and reality, the demanding, manipulative, inconsiderate, self-centered, and arrogant behavior of the narcissist can cause problems not only for themselves but also for all people his or her life.

Machiavellianism

Strictly defined, Machiavellianism is the political philosophy of Niccolò Machiavelli, who lived from 1469 until 1527 in Italy. In contemporary society, Machiavellianism is a term used to describe the popular understanding of people who are perceived as displaying very high political or professional ambitions. In psychology, however, the Machiavellianism scale is used to measure the degree to which people with deviant personalities say manipulative behavior.

Machiavelli wrote The Prince, a political treatise. He stated that sincerity, honesty, and other virtues were indeed admirable qualities. In politics, the capacity to engage in deceit, betrayal, and other forms of criminal behavior was acceptable if there were no other means of achieving political aims to protect one's interests.

Popular misconceptions reduce this entire philosophy to the view that "the end justifies the means." To be fair, Machiavelli himself insisted that the more critical part of this equation was ensuring the end itself must first be justified. Furthermore, it is better to achieve such ends using means devoid of treachery whenever possible because there is less risk to the actor's interests.

Thus, seeking the most effective means of achieving a political end may not necessarily lead to the most treacherous. Also, not all political fortunes that have been justified as worth pursuing must be pursued. In many cases, the mere threat that a particular course of action may be followed may be enough to achieve that end. In some cases, the betrayal may be as mild as making a credible threat to take action that is not intended.

In contemporary society, many people overlook the fact that Machiavellianism is part of the "Dark Triad" of dark psychology and tacitly approve of the deviant behavior of political and business leaders who can amass great power or wealth. However, as a psychological disorder, Ma- Machiavellianism is entirely different from a chosen path to political power.

The person displaying Machiavellian personality traits does not consider whether his or her actions are. The most effective means of achieving their goals, whether there are alternatives that do not involve deceit or treachery, or even whether the ultimate result of his or her actions is worth achieving. The Machiavellian personality is not evidence of a strategic or calculating mind attempting to reach a worthwhile objective in a contentious environment. Instead, it is always on, whether the situation calls for a cold, calculating, and manipulative approach or not.

For example, we had all called in sick to work when we just wanted a day off. But for most of us, such conduct is not how we usually behave. After such acts of dishonesty, many of us feel guilty. Those who display a high degree of Machiavellianism would not just lie when they want a day off; they see lying and dishonesty as the only way to conduct themselves in all situations, regardless of whether doing so results in any benefit.

What's more, because of the degree of social acceptance and tacit approval granted to Machiavellian personalities who successfully attain political power, their presence in society does not receive the kind of negative attention accorded to the other two members of the Dark Triad—psychopathy and narcissism.

Psychopathy

Psychopathy is defined as a mental disorder with several identifying characteristics: antisocial behavior, amorality, an inability to develop empathy, establish meaningful personal relationships, extreme egocentricity, and recidivism, with repeated violations resulting from an apparent failure to learn from the consequences of earlier transgressions. In turn, antisocial behavior is defined as behavior based upon a goal of violating formal and/or informal rules of social conduct through criminal activity or through acts of personal, private protest, or opposition, all of which are directed against other individuals' society in general.

Egocentricity is the behavior when the offending person sees himself or herself as the central focus of the world, or at least of all dominant social and political activity. Empathy is the ability to view and understand events, thoughts, emotions, and beliefs from others' perspectives. It is considered one of the most essential psychological components for establishing successful, ongoing relationships.

Amorality is entirely different from immorality. An immoral act is an act that violates established moral codes. An immoral person can be confronted with his or her actions with the expectation that they will recognize that their actions are offensive from a moral, if not a legal, standpoint. Amorality, on the other hand, represents psychology that does not realize that any moral codes exist, or if they do, that they have no value in determining whether or not to act in one way or another.

Thus, someone displaying psychopathy may commit horrendous acts that cause tremendous psychological and physical trauma and not ever understand that what he or she has done is wrong. Worse still, those who display signs of psychopathy usually worsen over time because they cannot connect the problems in their lives and the lives of those in the world around them and their own harmful and destructive actions.

The Dark Triad in Practice

The professional workplace has acknowledged the presence of people exhibiting Dark Triad characteristics.

The following diagram illustrates that they are tolerated for their efficiency and their ability to get things done but contrasts that ability with the adverse effects it has on their ability to form personal relationships:

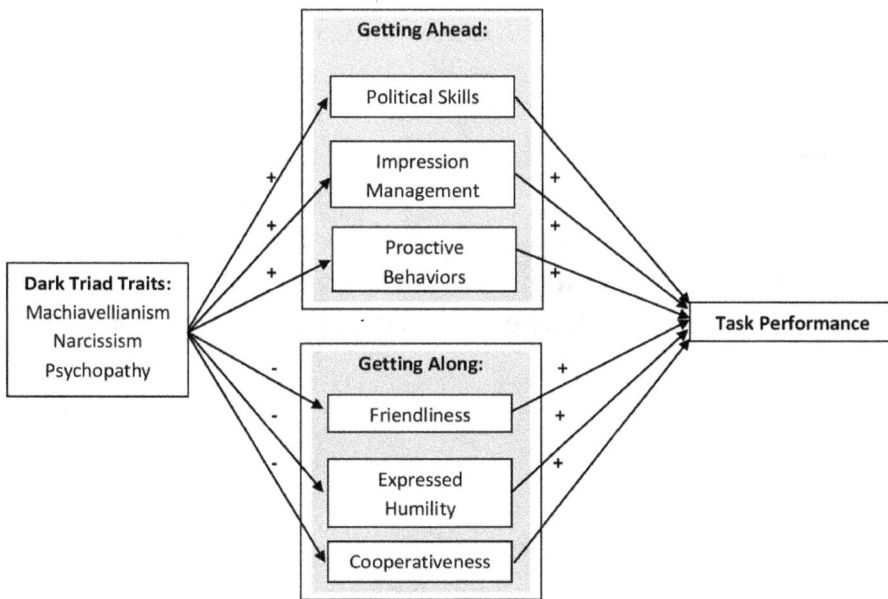

(Benjamin McLarty, Mississippi State University, 2015)

The remainder will discuss a wide variety of people and situations where you may find one, two, all three, or some combination of these Dark Triad personalities working in concert around you.

The clinical descriptions are easy enough to categorize. In isolation, it can be reasonably straightforward to separate one type of dark psychology from another. The real world is a lot messier. Many of us have grown accustomed to so-called "toxic relationships," whether they are relationships with our partners, co-workers, family members, bosses, or political and community leaders.

Also, dark psychology manifestations are often far more mundane than the dramatic examples we see in major television and film productions about serial killers and other criminals' romantic lives. The more we accept these relationships, as usual, the more difficult it will be to identify them as problematic.

Remember that psychological, emotional, and social predators do not think of themselves as sick. Their lack of morality and empathy, and their adaption from a very early age to live according to rules and methods you may find wrong, can make their presence intimidating. However, you should also remember that even when their amorality and lack of empathy may allow them to enjoy it. An unfair advantage in relationships, their mental capacities result from underdevelopment, not a higher evolutionary state.

Chapter 29. The Dark Triad

The dark triad is a psychology term that refers to a person's behavioral characteristics, which is, in most cases, defined as narcissism, Machiavellianism, and psychopathy. Some people rate it as a mental disorder and some as a disaster that just dawns on someone changing their behavior and how they relate to others. Dark triad generally affects a person's personality, making them take advantage of others. People with these traits tend to be manipulative, deceptive, and egoistic. They attempt to brainwash others to gain success and fame.

Politicians are, on most occasions, the worst group of people affected by this personality disorder. Their lives are full of lies, ego, and manipulation. To gain power, most of them only deceive other people to get public support and seem successful. Many people fall victim to the dark triad because they are not well exposed to the point of understanding what it is. They cannot easily tell when this is being used against them.

Persons with dark triad personalities have no empathy for others. They always attempt to have everything for themselves, ignoring other people's importance around them. Narcissists still want to be regarded as the most influential people in society. They want to be praised and admired all the time, a kind of behavior that only manipulates others for the benefit of their interests.

You may be tempted to think that these people are insane. From my perspective to some extent, they are. No one in his normal state of mind would want to have everything go their side at the expense of others. To these people who possess a Machiavellianism trait, they always want to win and be declared successful. They go as far as deceiving everyone around them to turn out the right person. They easily exploit the "less fortunate" in society to open their ways.

Apart from politicians, bloggers are another group of people that are overwhelmed by these traits. For example, in Kenya, we have Dr. Miguna, who is all over the social media busy manipulating people—the youth and young politicians being the most affected. He tries to make everyone his psychopath through his blogs, twits, books, and constant drama here and there.

Can we Say Dr. Miguna is insane? He is all over seeking fame and wants everyone to believe he is always right, and the rest are wrong. He manipulates everyone, and those who follow his steps end up being disappointed at the end. Once he gets what he is looking for, he turns against you and uses your negatives to manipulate others that are not in the same line as him. He comes up with dramas to attract attention and convince everyone to believe whatever he does.

While politicians everywhere are fighting him back, the youth become psychos by his blogs and believe that he is right because he is fighting politicians whom he claims to be narcissists. Not to be personal, I would like to say that if you research deeply into psychology, you will find most bloggers with the same interest showing narcissism, Machiavellianism, and psychopathy traits. They won't feel guilty or ashamed because they don't even notice that they are too much.

Anyone can be a victim of these traits. You may, at one point in your life, find yourself in a relationship with a narcissist. Before you notice it, you will be exploited and used by your partner. Your partner can be that antagonistic person that only feels superior to you and those around you. They will always want to be treated special and can exploit you to serve their interests. They often interact in a way that shows you are less important and not as good as them.

This kind of person usually wants to be listened to. They will prefer seeking attention than empathizing with you or even recognizing your needs. Everything they do is always for their benefit. They only concentrate on feeling better in the relationship and are never ready to give you a listening year. You have no say in their decisions because this makes them feel less important to you and don't respect their decisions.

To know that you are in a relationship with a narcissist, you will realize that your partner doesn't really care about how you feel. They only expect you to make them happy and superior without considering what you go through for them to be what they want. Failing to meet their interests makes them feel so low and unwanted in the relationship. They make you feel like you are of no good to them and that you don't deserve them.

They can also be antisocial and low self-esteemed. They will always think of their mistakes as the worst ever and that none can be compared. Whenever they fail in something, they will feel like they don't fit in society anymore and imperfect. They feel so drowned and depressed as a result of one mistake. This is always brought about by the fear of being a normal person.

On some occasions, narcissists attempt to praise themselves too much without realizing how majestic they can be. They never stop talking about their achievements and plans in life. They always talk about how intelligent and successful they are and even exaggerate what they are capable of. They always want people to believe that their success cannot be related to someone else's. Stopping them from doing this makes them feel stupid, and they can easily hate you for pinpointing their imperfections.

These persons' living standards are always set high by them, which is becoming realistic because they are in a way that has low standards. Their lives are usually filled with a fantasy about success, and they expect everyone around them to respect them because their destinies are thought to be successful. No one can ever change their perception in their minds without hurting them and making them feel useless.

At some point, these people are always depressed, and no one will ever understand the reason for their depression. Understanding them becomes difficult. If you are not a psychologist, you will always be brainwashed to serve their interests before noticing what you are getting yourself into. Other people can advise you, but you will not have the time to listen to what they have to say because you will have fallen victim to narcissism. The narcissist will, by that time, have full control of you.

You are always left torn between thoughts when it reaches a point that you no longer understand a friend or a partner who has a dark personality. Failing to listen to them makes them feel worse than other people while listening to you is useless to them, on the other hand. They never have time to listen to you but to seek the audience all the time.

Machiavellian leaders are the most dangerous leaders because they are always cunning and duplicitous. They always manipulate everyone from doing what they want, whether they like it or not, and never reveal any reason for their actions. They only do that when the favor is on their side. They always make people believe that they are the most intelligent and that no one's intelligence can be compared to theirs. Those who believe in this kind of leaders are never ready to listen to other people's advice unless they align with the Machiavellian heads.

Dark triad strikes too much due to several reasons and the following additional reasons.

1. The Understanding of Dark Triad Is Not Everybody's Cup of Tea

Not everyone has the psychology of understanding dark personality. This leads to many of us fall victim to dark triads without noticing it. We get manipulated easily and exploited to serve the interest of narcissists and Machiavellian leaders without a choice of thinking a second time or even the chance to take an alternative move.

2. The Fear of Standing Alone

Narcissists always manipulate the big number from being on their side and supporting their ideas. This has left many people stranded between thoughts because they fear being left alone for making an opposing decision. They fear of not getting back up from those around you led many people to fall, victims of the dark triad since they are forced to take steps they were not ready to take.

This usually happens with people who are often close to this kind of person or whose friends are involved with those with dark personalities.

3. I Don't Want to Lose a Friend

Many people tend to value friendship more than their own safety. They are too much into their friend's decisions and way of life that they even forget they are also important. Such people are the most common victims of the dark triad. They easily get exploited by their friends into doing what their friends want, what makes them happy.

In this case, when you're are friends with a narcissist, then you have no choice. You will always be a tool for happiness. You will be ready to listen to all sorts of boasting and exaggerated stories from your friends.

4. Investing Your Trust in the Wrong Person

On many occasions, we don't always know the right person to trust. Laying your trust in someone without considering their personality opens a gate for you to be used by narcissists. This normally occurs in relationships that are just beginning, and partners wish to travel miles away together.

Many fall into traps of their partners because they invest too much trust in them that they can never think of the negative side of them. This is what makes the narcissists overjoyed and leave them feeling so highly of themselves.

5. Believing Too Fast

These narcissists always have their stories told everywhere by them and by those who believe helplessly in them. They always catch the interests of those who believe in all stories they are told because they believe the people telling the story are always right, intelligent, and successful.

The narcissist always catches others' attention with their striking success that makes others believe in them desperately and follow their steps blindly without a third eye to see into the future and the consequences of following these people.

6. Most People Don't Care

The tendency of assuming everything said by those in authority is final is what makes us victims of manipulation and exploitation. Some of us don't even care about what is going on around them, and having no idea about it for them is even much better. Some say that something you don't know does not hurt.

People with dark personalities easily exploit such people because they know the favor will always be on their side no matter what. No one will stand against them because they don't even care in the first place.

7. Psychopathy

Being too possessed with someone is what leads you to become their psychopaths. You will always want to listen to what they say, and at the end of it, you will be convinced they are right, and anything said against them is wrong. You will feel pain when they are in pain are depressed when they are depressed because you have become their shadow. Whoever sees you see the person you have invested your personality in.

Conclusion

Now that you've learned some of the basic dark psychology disciplines, you have a great deal more power than you had before. At the very least, you will be better able to recognize controlling techniques and behaviors when other people try to use them against you. If someone is trying to manipulate or even persuade you, you can now see through their tricks and resist.

But you also have the unique opportunity to use dark psychology for your personal growth and improvement. Just because these tools and techniques are labeled 'dark' doesn't mean they're inherently destructive. Many techniques, including hypnosis and NLP, were first developed as self-improvement tools. Only when people learned how to turn these techniques against other people did they become relegated to the field of 'dark' psychology.

NLP, persuasion techniques, body language, and even hypnosis are all regularly taught in social spheres that we would not normally consider 'dark.' Athletes, business people, teachers and educators, actors, entertainers, and marketers all regularly use these techniques to improve their performance, increase their productivity, make themselves better negotiators, and yes, to convince others to do what they want. There's nothing inherently amoral about social influence, especially if the thing you're persuading the other person to do is good for them. Using NLP techniques to persuade your alcoholic partner to get help is hardly an act of evil or manipulation. Neither is learning to read your teenager's body language to improve your communication and defuse potential conflict.

With great power, however, does come great responsibility. Whenever you decide to employ any of these techniques against another person, always take a step back and ask yourself, "What are the consequences for the other person if I get my desired outcome? Will the other person be hurt? Will this put them in danger? Will this compromise their core values or beliefs in some way?" If the answer to any of these three questions is yes, you have to find another way to get what you want without manipulating tactics. All of the techniques that you've learned are extremely powerful. With patience and practice, they do work. Suppose you become skilled in any of these disciplines and decide to use them for the wrong reasons. In that case, you could cause some serious damage to another person's psychological well-being and risk losing your important relationships if someone else becomes aware of what you're doing.

I hope that, you re-enter your life as a more secure and empowered person. Psychological techniques are subtle and often context-based. It's normal to be clumsy when you first begin, and you should always be aware of how the other person is responding so that you can make necessary and appropriate adjustments to your techniques.

With these tactics at your disposal, you are no longer at the mercy of other people. If you find yourself constantly rubbing other people the wrong way, perhaps receiving labels like 'bossy' or 'pushy,' you now have a variety of subtler ways to get what you want. If you're someone that's constantly fighting and barreling over others, you know that sometimes being straightforward isn't the best option. Being too blunt can often backfire on you. Asking for what you need more subtly won't only get you more success in life—it may even make it easier for you to build healthy relationships with other people.

If you find yourself in the opposite position, these tactics can work for you, too. If you feel that you're just too timid to get what you want or find yourself easily pushed around by other people, you now have a way to succeed. Instead of running headlong into conflicts that scare you, you can try a different approach, one that may feel much more comfortable. As you start to achieve results, you'll probably feel a big improvement in your confidence. And the more confident you feel, the more comfortable you will be with straightforward communication, making you a much better communicator all the way around.

Most importantly of all, now that you are aware of dark psychology, those who would wish to do you harm have significantly less power over you. Suppose someone does try to manipulate, persuade, or use NLP against you in the future. In that case, you will be better able to recognize their tactics before something bad happens. And suppose you are currently in a relationship with a manipulative person. In that case, you now have a better idea of their tactics and therefore take steps to free yourself from their influence.

www.ingramcontent.com/pod-product-compliance
Lightning Source LLC
Chambersburg PA
CBHW060335030426
42336CB00011B/1356